CW01642769

Crossing the Minch

Exploring the Links between Skye and the Outer Hebrides

The Proceedings of a two day Conference held in Skye on 4th and 5th May 2007

The Islands Book Trust

LIVING HISTORY

THE ISLANDS BOOK TRUST
URRAS LEABHRAICHEAN NAN EILEAN

Published in 2008 by The Islands Book Trust

www.theislandsbooktrust.com

Copyright of the individual chapters remains with the named authors. Other than brief extracts for the purpose of review, no part of this publication may be reproduced in any form without the written consent of the publisher and copyright owner.

© The Islands Book Trust 2008

ISBN: 978-0-9555420-3-9

All rights reserved. No part of this publication may be reproduced, stored in a retrieval system, or transmitted in any other form or by any means, electronic, mechanical, photocopying, recording or otherwise without the prior written permission of the publishers. This book may not be lent, hired out, resold or otherwise disposed of by way of trade in any form of binding or cover other than that in which it is published, without the prior consent of the publishers.

The Islands Book Trust
10 Callicvol
Port of Ness
Isle of Lewis
HS2 0XA
Tel: 01851 820946

Printed and bound by Strath Print, Isle of Skye

Cover photographs courtesy of Cailean Maclean

© Cailean Maclean

Price £9.00

CONTENTS

John Randall – Introduction and Conclusions 4

Aonghas MacCoinnich – Sìol Torcuil and their Lordship in the Sixteenth Century 7

Anne Frater – Màiri Nighean Alasdair Ruaidh 33

Bill Lawson – Migration Links between Skye and the Outer Hebrides 50

Iain Mac an Tàilleir – Where do People Speak Gaelic? – Skye and the Western Isles? 60

Roger Hutchinson – Sporting Links between Skye and The Outer Hebrides 70

INTRODUCTION AND CONCLUSIONS

John Randall

This publication covers contributions to the Book Trust's first ever event in Skye, which was held on 4th-5th May 2007 in the dramatic surroundings of Sabhal Mor Ostaig, the Gaelic college. The Outer Hebrides were represented by people from Lewis, Harris, Scalpay, and Benbecula, while from the other side of the Minch were many Sgiathanaich, together with residents of Raasay, Glasgow, Edinburgh, and Galway. We heard six outstanding presentations – from Domhnall Uilleam Stiubhart, Aonghas MacCoinnich, Anne Frater, Iain Mac an Tàilleir, Roger Hutchinson, and Bill Lawson on subjects as diverse as the poetry of Màiri nighean Alasdair Ruaidh, and why shinty is not a major sport in the Western Isles. Five of these are included in this volume. We were also treated to some wonderful photographs from both sides of the Minch by Cailean Maclean, and I am delighted that some of these have also been reproduced here.

Like all Book Trust events, the conference sought to bring people together from different backgrounds, both geographically and in other ways, in order to learn from each other's perspectives and maybe re-examine conventional thinking. So huge is the subject of links between Skye and the Outer Hebrides that the conference 'Crossing the Minch' could equally well have been called 'Scratching the Surface'. The Book Trust is keen to follow up with further events which explore the similarities and differences between these two remarkable areas whose history has been intertwined over the centuries. We were greatly encouraged by the quality of the contributions to the Sabhal Mor event, and would like to thank everyone involved at the college for making this such a special occasion. I hope that this volume will enable the contributions to reach a wider audience, and stimulate more thought, debate, and research on trans-Minch issues.

What comes across strongly from the earlier contributions is the strength of historic links across the Minch – a name which Domhnall Uilleam Stiubhart suggested may have been derived from the French 'La Manche', given the extensive use of the area for by French, Dutch, and English, as well as Scottish, fishermen. These links were partly derived from clan and land ownership connections, with a number of territories (eg those of the Macleods of Lewis, the Macleods of Dunvegan and Harris, the Macdonalds of Sleat and North Uist, and Clanranald) spanning parts of the Outer Hebrides, Skye, and indeed the mainland.

Aonghas MacCoinnich's detailed account of Sìol Torcail (the branch of the Macleod family which owned both Lewis and Vaternish in Skye, along with Raasay and parts of the mainland in Assynt and Coigeach) illustrates the complex pattern of rivalries and alliances which led in the early 17th century to the Mackenzies taking over ownership of Lewis, and also controlling Macleod of Dunvegan and Macdonald of Sleat. That this was achieved with Royal support, following the failure of the Fife Adventurers plantation scheme, indicates not only the Scottish Crown's desire for political control in the area but also the economic importance of the Minch fishery.

Land rights, and family kinship, on both sides of the Minch also provide the background to the many uncertainties concerning the life of the renowned 17th century Gaelic bardess Màiri nighean Alasdair Ruadh, which are explored by Anne Frater. The fact that the family of Sir Norman Macleod of Berneray held tacks both on Harris and Skye may, as Bill Lawson points out, explain some of the confusion about in which area Màiri spent most of her life and to which chief she held allegiance – a long-standing dispute which Anne Frater believes should be concluded in favour of Harris on the basis of careful sifting of the available evidence.

Bill Lawson's masterful survey of migration links across the Minch highlights the significance of the movement of tacksmen and their families across the Minch from one part of a chief's estate to another up to the early 19th century (for example, the Dingwall family which moved from one part of Macdonald of Sleat's lands in Skye to another part in North Uist). But with the decline in the tack system, this migration also seems to have declined, as indicated by the small number of people resident in Skye in 1851 who had been born in the Outer Hebrides. By the mid-nineteenth century, common economic problems were leading to large-scale emigration from both sides of the Minch – but while the Outer Hebrides looked largely across the Atlantic, Skye emigrants tended to move more to the cities of the mainland.

So up to perhaps the nineteenth century, the sea was more of a link than a barrier, and movement across the Minch was relatively common. A shared cultural heritage emerged, shaped by language and kinship, but subject in the eighteenth and nineteenth centuries to common economic and social pressures, with clearance, the land struggle, and planned resettlement in some areas (including one trans-Minch scheme in the 1920s which brought families from Harris and Lewis to the Portnalong area of Skye).

But changing economic circumstances and transport links seem to have led to the Minch becoming more of a barrier during the 19th century. Indeed, it appears from Roger Hutchinson's fascinating account of the history of shinty that the costs and inconvenience of crossing the Minch regularly was a major reason why this quintessentially Gaelic sport declined in the Outer Hebrides heartland of Gaelic as greater centralisation in the organisation of the sport developed.

Today, despite technological advances, the sea is probably even more of a barrier, and in some ways links are less close – typified perhaps by the post-1975 Comhairle nan Eilean Siar which has brought about new connections within the Outer Hebrides, which to some extent are replacing the previous local government links across the Minch of Ross and Cromarty and Inverness-shire, which had so many repercussions, for example through the school system.

Nonetheless, both sides of the Minch remain subject to similar pressures – as Iain Mac an Tàilleir's detailed and alarming report on the changing status of Gaelic emphasises. He notes, for example, that in 2001 the percentage of Gaelic-speaking pre-school children in Lewis and Harris (31.5%) was very close to the percentage of Gaelic speakers among the total population of Skye (31.1%), an indication perhaps that unless trends change radically Lewis and Harris could soon be where Skye is today in relation to Gaelic.

In conclusion, it is clear that there is enormous potential to share experiences and learn from the histories of the two island groups across the Minch. There are so many topics which would repay comparative examination, of which just a few are listed below:

- The activities of the early Christian church, and the extent of links in the pre-Viking Age.
- Place-name similarities and differences in relation to Norse, Gaelic, and English, and the light this sheds on population and cultural patterns.
- Skye and the Outer Hebrides during the period of the Lordship of the Isles.
- The Minch at the time of the Jacobite Risings.
- The impact of the Reformation and later Church development such as the Evangelical Movement, the Disruption, and religious revivals.
- Attempts to stimulate fishing development and the kelp industry based on the resources of the Minch.
- Other unsuccessful industrial development schemes, such as diatomite, marble, and iron ore in Skye and Raasay, and the Lewis Chemical Works and Lord Leverhulme's plans across the Minch.
- The comparative impact of the Clearances, the Land Struggle, and the resettlement schemes of the early 20th century.
- Population trends today, and the future of Gaelic and other aspects of traditional culture.

I very much hope that through the Book Trust and other means there will be an opportunity to explore some of these themes in the future, and that this volume will act as a spur to more comparative history by demonstrating the rich potential of such an approach.

SÌOL TORCAIL AND THEIR LORDSHIP IN THE SIXTEENTH CENTURY

Aonghas MacCoinnich

Had there been newspaper headlines during the sixteenth century, the Macleods of Lewis would have figured prominently on the front pages, and had these been red-top tabloids, the exploits of the thrice married Ruairidh MacLeòid, who fathered some four sons by his three wives and a further five sons outwith wedlock would certainly have kept them interested. Under the leadership of Ruairidh, the last undisputed chief (c.1538-95), they were perennial rebels, and rarely in good favour in parts south and east of the kingdom of Scotland. Ruairidh's late uncle Torcail (†c.1506), the former chief, had succumbed to a royally sanctioned expedition at the opening of the sixteenth century, involving a fleet which reduced Stornoway castle with cannon. Ruairidh himself was to continue this pattern of defiance to the dictats of Edinburgh and came under sustained and serious pressure towards the middle of the century and again towards the end of the sixteenth century from the Crown and their agents.[1]

The Macleods of Lewis just after old Ruairidh's death suffered what Hollywood scriptwriters (think asteroid disaster movies) like to call 'an extinction level event' in terms of the Fife plantation (1598-1609) and the subsequent invasion by the Mackenzies of Kintail (1609-11). There is no room to explore this process in detail here other than to offer a brief summary of their political history in the first section of the paper, some of which offers fresh primary material, and much of which paraphrases subject matter covered comprehensively in W.C. Mackenzie's *History of the Outer Hebrides*.[2] The second section will consider the composition of the lordship in terms of personnel and with an eye to geography before finally taking a look at some of the wider questions arising from this. Why did this happen to the Macleods, and, why is this 'Lewis' 'clan' the subject of discussion in a paper at a conference whose theme focuses on the links between Skye and the Outer Isles? Hopefully by exploring the nature of some aspects of the Macleod lordship in the sixteenth century and its demise some valuable light can be shed on both the reasons underlying the friction between the Macleods of Lewis and their countrymen, and the same discussion can contribute to the consideration of the nature of the linkages between An t-Eilean Sgitheanach (Skye) and Eilean Leòdhais (Lewis) during the sixteenth century.

---

1 Modern Gaelic forms of personal names, such as *Ruairidh, Torcail, Dòmhnall Dubh, Coinneach* have been privileged here for the purposes of this paper rather than 'Rory / Rodrick' and 'Torquil / Torkill,' 'Donald dow,' 'Kenneth / Kennoch' and their variants. *Sìol Torcail* similarly has been adopted throughout in preference to 'Shiell Torkill' and its variant spellings. Various forms have been adopted for 'surnames' and placenames.

2 Chapter 5-8 in Mackenzie's book (Paisley 1903) still offers the best and most detailed treatment of this period. See also D. Gregory, *History of the Western Highlands and Isles of Scotland from A.D. 1493 to A.D. 1625* (1832: 2nd edition, Glasgow 1881, reprinted by John Donald, 1974).

I

The Macleods, from their very earliest appearances on historical record sometime in the fourteenth century, were split into two main groups: Sìol Tormoid (The Macleods of Harris and Dunvegan in Skye) who continued to exist as an entity, and Sìol Torcail (The Macleods of Lewis), who, with the exception of cadets such as Raasay and Assynt were eradicated as a cohesive force by the opening decade of the seventeenth century.[3] Why the Macleods of Lewis then, where were they and why take time to consider such a long extinct group? No one would seriously challenge the status of the Macleods of Harris/Dunvegan as a fairly important clan in this period, not perhaps in the same league as the Campbells (few if any were) in terms of importance, not perhaps as powerful as the Mackenzies were to become by 1600, but a significant group of players nonetheless, on a par, perhaps, with the MacLeans before their downfall in the late seventeenth century, or the Macdonalds of Sleat towards the end of the sixteenth century. However for two to three hundred years the Macleods of Lewis were arguably an equal if not larger and more formidable organisation than their namesakes in Harris and Dunvegan.

Sìol Torcail had been one of a number of powerful clan groups within the Macdonald Lordship of the Isles between the later fourteenth century and the disintegration of this Lordship, 1475-93. The Macdonald lordship collapsed due to a mixture of internal disunity and pressure from James III & James IV, culminating in the forfeiture of the Lordship in 1493. James IV attempted to extend his control in the area and by so doing maximise his revenues, an approach continued by his successors with varying degrees of success. James essentially promoted divide and rule with a carrot and stick approach. Former vassals of the Macdonalds (including Macdonald cadets such as MacIain of Ardnamurchan) were granted new charters holding their lands as tenants in chief of the Crown rather than as vassals of the Macdonald Lords of the Isles. However, for reasons which are not always clear, families such as the Macleods of Lewis (and others, led by various septs of the Macdonalds) were extremely unhappy with the new order and continued to try and rebel to reinstate the former Macdonald Lordship for much of the sixteenth century. Although the last 'serious' pro-lordship rising is usually stated to have been that of 1545, it remained a live issue, at least in the minds of many Macdonald septs, for another century. This is one of the wider contexts in which the Macleods of Lewis, who controlled the northern end of this lordship, operated.[4]

---

3 'Mcleoid of Lewes together with his trybe the Shiell Torquill,' in 'The Ewill Trowbles of the Lewes' (c.1630) pp. 265-279 in J.R.N. MacPhail, ed., *Highland Papers ii* (Edinburgh, 1916) at p. 279. For the origins of the Macleods see, W. Matheson, 'The Macleods of Lewis' (320-337) in TGSI 51, 1976-78; W.D.H. Sellar, 'The Ancestry of the Macleods reconsidered' (233-58) in TGSI 60, 2000.

4 Bannerman, J., 'The Lordship of the Isles' (209-240) in J. Brown, ed. Scottish Society in the Fifteenth Century (London 1977); D. Gregory, *History of the Western Highlands and Isles of Scotland*

Rebellion, 1502-1506

Although Torcail Macleod of Lewis had been granted a charter of Lewis by James IV in 1498, by 1502 he was declared a rebel. While James might not have felt the need to attend to this rebellion in person, Torcail was nevertheless a powerful, well-respected chief and his rebellion, like a rebellion by any other magnate in the kingdom, was not something James could afford to ignore. Torcail had been married to Katherine, a daughter of the Earl of Argyll (the Chancellor) sometime around 1498-c.1508 and, seemingly to a daughter of Macdonald of Islay who was a widow of Macdonald of Sleat.[5] His nephew, the teenage Dòmhnall Dubh (Macdonald) the grandson and heir of John the last Lord of the Isles, escaped from custody in Argyll to Macleod's castle in Stornoway.[6] Torcail supported an attempt by the Macdonalds to reinstate the Lordship of the Isles in the person of his nephew, something the king was not prepared to countenance.[7] James ordered a fleet up to the Isles to reduce the rebellion. The Earl of Huntly led the force against Lewis with a contingent of ships, including the 'Raven' which, with cannon, helped reduce Stornoway Castle in 1506. This underlines a point made by Steve Boardman, that the stone fortresses of the isles were, due to the advances in artillery by the time of James IV's reign, no longer impregnable, and that no part of the kingdom could defy

---

from A.D. 1493 to A.D. 1625 (2nd ed. Glasgow, 1881); D. U. Stiùbhart, *Rìoghachd nan Eilean* (Dùn Bhlathain, 2005) 118-123. Although clans such as the Macleans were frequently in rebellion, they were also quite prepared to deal with Edinburgh when required. Lachlan Maclean of Duart in a petitione to the Lords of Council (May 1517), referred to his erstwhile allies, the Macdonalds as 'the wykyt blud of the ylis, for als long as that blud rengis [reigns] the king sal nevir hayf the Ylis in pace when tha s[e]e thar tyme to brek as it is dayly knawne.' R. K. Hannay, ed., *Acts of the Lords of the Council in Public Affairs, 1501-1554* (Edinburgh, 1932) 88. Gregory, *History of the Western Highlands*, 115-122; Mackenzie, *History of the Outer Hebrides*, 124-6. For a recent view of the Macleod lordship in a wider context see A. Halford-Macleod, 'The Macleods of Lewis... and of Assynt, Coigach and Gairloch' (193-213) in J.R. Baldwin, ed., *Peoples and Settlement in North-West Ross* (Aberdeen, 1994).

5 For a discussion of the marriages see A. Morrison & D. Mackinnon, The Macleods- *The Genealogy of a Clan* (5 vols. Edinburgh, 1968-1976) iv, p. 32-5; Boardman, *The Campbells*, 273, 283; Mackenzie, *History of the Outer Hebrides*, 120-123. Morrison (& Mackinnon) follow Mackenzie (p.123) in stating (p. 4) that Katherine Campbell, sister of Gilleasbuig was the second wife of Torcail, (married 1498). However, Torcail was probably dead by 1511 if not earlier, and in a document dated 27 July 1508, Katherine Campbell still styled herself 'Lady Lewis,' and used her husband's seal for a document. *AT iii*, 85. This suggests that Torcail was married first to the unnamed Macdonald woman. She may have predeceased Catherine Campbell, who was thus probably his second wife. A Gaelic praise poem to him was still circulating in Campbell country and written down some years after his death. W.J. Watson, ed., *Scottish Verse from the Book of the Dean of Lismore* (SGTS, Edinburgh, 1978) 100-104, 281-2.

6 Boardman has suggested that this might have been a fosterage arrangement, c. 1498, made with the consent of the Campbells before Torcail rebelled. S. Boardman, *The Campbells*, 1250-1513 (Edinburgh, 2006) 273, 283.

7 Forfeiture of 'Torcule Makloid of the Lewis' (24 December 1505). *APS ii*, 263-4; Mackenzie, *History of the Outer Hebrides*, 110-123.

the monarch with impunity.[8] After this Torcail seems to have disappeared (missing, presumed dead) and his conquered lordship was administered by Andrew Stewart Bishop of Caithness (James's man of business in Ross and the north) who, together with Alasdair Crotach of Dunvegan seem to have administered the Sìol Torcail lands between 1506 and 1511.[9]

From Dynastic Manoeuvring to Rebellion, 1538-9

The succession then took a peculiar twist (see family tree, appendix C) in that Malcolm, Torcail's brother, took control of the inheritance of the chiefship of the Macleods of Lewis, to the exclusion of John mac Torcail his nephew, and this was endorsed by the Crown. This lasted until Malcolm's death in 1528 at which time his nephew, John mac Torcail with backing from his mother's people the Macdonalds of Sleat, was powerful enough to seize the chiefship to the exclusion of Malcolm's son and heir, Ruairidh. This coincided with wider Crown attempts to assert their authority in the Isles in this period.[10] John mac Torcail, the son of a chief whose last recorded attitudes to the Crown had been defiance, was unlikely to have been viewed with particular favour by officials at the Stewart court, and it is likely (even if a little ironic given his career over the subsequent decades) that the Crown may have sanctioned the seizure of the Macleod of Lewis chiefship by Ruairidh mac Malcolm (Gille Caluim) after John's death sometime around 1538. The date of Ruairidh's accession to the chiefship coincided with a serious rebellion in the Western Isles in 1539. The Mackenzies, who had been exercising the crown's power in the region, and in the process extending their own power and influence, acted as the lightning rod for the rebels, the perennially disaffected Macdonalds, led at this time by Dòmhnall Gorm (Macdonald) of Sleat who died besieging the Mackenzie stronghold, Eilean Donan castle, 1539-40. Sìol Torcail played a prominent role in this rebellion which also included Alasdair Crotach (Macleod) of Dunvegan, Cameron of Lochiel and Macneil of Barra. Although the siege was unsuccessful, the surrounding Mackenzie lands of Wester Ross were targeted and wasted as the 'rebellious' clans, Ruairidh Macleod of Lewis foremost among them, retaliated against those wielding crown authority.[11]

---

8 TA iii, 340. Boardman, *The Campbells*, 268.

9 A. MacCoinnich, *Tùs gu Iarlachd: Eachdraidh Chlann Choinnich c. 1466-1637* (Tràchdas PhD, Oilthigh Obar Dheathain, 2004) 139-140. Torcail may still have been alive in 1508 as his wife was using his seal in Dunoon, resigning lands to her brother, the Earl of Argyll. *Argyll Transcripts iii*, 85.

10 Archibald 'Gillespick Roy Oig' Campbell 4th Earl of Argyll was to spearhead the Crown offensive south of Ardnamurchan (south isles) and James Stewart earl of Moray was to manage government pressure in the north isles (Hebrides north and west of Ardnamurchan). Hannay, ed., *Acts of the Lords of Council in Public Affairs*, 358. J. Cameron, *James V, 228-248*. For the 'north Isles' see W.F. Skene, ed., *Celtic Scotland, A History of Ancient Alban* (Edinburgh, 1880) iii, 428.

11 RSS ii, no 3943, p. 597-8; Gregory, *Western Highlands*, 145; Mackenzie, *History of the Outer Hebrides*, 130-131.

Extension of Royal Control

This rebellion failed and the consequences of this failure must have been keenly felt in the isles. Although King James V's visit to and the supposed renaming of Port Rìgh (Portree) is better remembered, both Kintail and Stornoway were key stopping places in his voyage of 1540.[12] James, like his father, followed the tried and trusted route of coercion leavened with reward. James V's coercion was more proactive than his father's. Whereas James IV had used nobles to do his bidding against Torcail Macleod in 1505, James V was present in person and already had his own well-established clients in the area. The diversion James took to Kintail was no accident. James rewarded the Mackenzies of Kintail, already crown favourites (several of them were at court during the 1530s), by giving them increased powers and responsibilities in the west. John Mackenzie of Kintail was given the superiority of Glengarry's lands, and custody of Macdonald castles in Skye such as Dunscaith (Slèite) and possibly Duntulm in Tròndarnais to facilitate his role as royal baillie and enforcer.[13] A note in the records of the royal Treasurer, who, presumably had never heard of the place, illustrates the effect the Mackenzie presence was having. When a clerk in the treasury inserted the name 'Skye,' the scribe felt the need to qualify this by noting in the marginalia that this place was in the 'north Isles,' Skye being clearly a name royal accountants had been unfamiliar with.[14]

Rebellion, 1545-1555

This new tax-gathering initiative did little to win hearts and minds in the North Minch. Ruairidh Macleod of Lewis was again involved in a rising in support of the unfortunate Dòmhnall Dubh in 1545 in Dòmhnall's final attempt to re-instate the Lordship of the Isles. The Macleods of Lewis were prime movers in this as in every other serious attempt to resuscitate that Lordship.[15] While pardoned shortly afterwards, by the following decade Ruairidh's treasonable activities again exercised the minds of the regents in Edinburgh. After much deliberation, an expedition was despatched under the earls of Argyll and

12 May- June 1540. A.B. Taylor, I.H. Adams & G. Fortune eds., *Alexander Lindsay: A Rutter of the Scottish Seas circa 1540* (Greenwich, 1980) p. 14-15; J. Cameron, *James V*, 338; A. Nicolson, *History of Skye* (2nd ed., 1994) 36. However, the etymology of Port Rìgh was challenged by W.J. Watson, *The Celtic Placenames of Scotland* (1926: Birlinn ed., Edinburgh, 1993) p. 158, note 1.

13 A.L. Murray, ed., 'Accounts of the King's Pursemaster 1539-1540' (13-51) in *Miscellany of the Scottish History Society vol. X* (Edinburgh, 1965) at 40, 44, 46. *TA vi*, 92-3, 126; MacCoinnich, *Tùs gu Iarlachd*, 35, 161-2, 189-90. *ER xvii*, 342, 459, 492.

14 'The North Isles' were the name for the Hebrides north and west of Ardnamurchan in this period. *ER xvii*, 556. Skene, *Celtic Scotland iii*, 428.

15 Summons of treason and lese-majestie (9 September 1545) named 'Rodorik McCloid,' and his colleagues, some of whom were named as Macleod of Harris, and Clanranald. *APS ii*, 453, 455, 459, 465. It was probably no accident, as Mackenzie noted, that Macleod of Lewis was given pre-eminence in these processes of treason. Mackenzie, *History of the Outer Hebrides*, 143.

Atholl to bring him to heel in 1555.[16] A clue as to why Ruairidh's rebellion was being taken so seriously may lie in an earlier note of a commission from the regent James Duke of Châtelherault to the Earl of Argyll in 1551. In this Argyll was given a commission, 25 April 1551, to proceed against Lewis with all force necessary as 'Rory Macleod' of the Lews had taken a 'pupill' who he meant to use as a figurehead for a fresh pro-Macdonald / Lordship rebellion. The 'pupill' was un-named but might well have been the natural son left by the late Dòmhnall Dubh. Nothing more, in any case, was heard of this 'pupill' and by 1555 Ruairidh had made his peace with the government.[17]

A Dysfunctional Family?

The pattern of Ruairidh Macleod's marriages between c. 1535-1541, even if the dates and order of marriages is unclear, is significant in indicating crown and royal intent. Ruairidh seemingly married firstly Janet Mackenzie, which would fit with John Mackenzie's presence as a Crown baillie in the region sometime in the 1530s. The marriage between John's daughter Janet and Ruairidh of Lewis produced a son Torcail Conanach (c. 1530? –c. 1610). He was raised by his uncle John Mackenzie of Ord in Strathconon.[18] By December 1541, however, Ruairidh's first marriage to Janet had broken down, and he remarried to Barbara Stewart (a cousin of the king), daughter of Lord Avondale. Barbara was well-connected. Her father, himself a cousin of the king, had remarried Margaret Tudor, James V's widowed mother.[19] This shows that the Crown (who had an influence if not the gift of such marriages) were making an effort, post rebellion, to bring Ruairidh into the fold, albeit it did little to curb Ruairidh's rebellious tendencies, in the later 1540s and 1550s.[20] The couple had one son, also called Torcail, known

---

16 *TA x*, 268, 277-8, 286; *RPCS xiv*, 14. P.E. Ritchie, *Mary of Guise in Scotland, 1548-1560: A Political Career* (East Linton, 2002) 166.

17 Gregory, *History of the Western Islands and Highlands* (1881) 169-185; Mackenzie, *History of the Outer Hebrides* (1903) 139-147; '[…] Macleod of the Lews hes laitlie takin ane pupill barne callit (blank) son to (blank) and haldis him in nurissing and maintenance of purposs and mynd to mak and set him forwert at the uttirmost of his power to be Lord of the Isles and to using that name and draw sa mony as he may git of opinioun to that effect quhairof the samen be sufferit it wilbe the occasion of gret troubles and inconvenientis to us […]' From abstract commission, dated 25 April 1551 to Argyll signed by the governor, James Hamilton, Duke of Chatelherault. *AT v, 5.* Respite to Macleod, dated 28 September 1555. *RSS iv*, no. 3047, p. 536.

18 Torcail was still alive in 1612 when he resigned all his rights to Lewis over to Kenneth Mackenzie of Kintail. Torcail had son named John who was an adult by1580 (John was killed c. 1585), again suggesting that Torcail himself had been born in the 1530s. He was refered to as the 'umquhill' (late) Torcail in 1624. Aberdeen University Library *MS 3470/15/1/8*. Mackenzie, *History of the Outer Hebrides*, 148. NAS CC 19/1/1 fol. 22. MacCoinnich, *Tùs gu Iarlachd*, 152-6.

19 Mackenzie, *History of the Outer Hebrides*, 135. Morrison, *The Macleods- The Genealogy of a Clan*, iv, p. 32-56.

20 Ruairidh was involved in the Donald Dubh rebellion (1545-6), a continuing rebellion against the regent (1551-5), and the wasting of Orkney (1559). *RSS iii*, no. 2210, p. 356. *RSS iv*, no 3307, p. 589; The parish of Westray, Orkney, were unable to pay their taxes, 1559, as they claimed that: 'this

as Torcail Oighre (the heir). The throwing over of Torcail Conanach the eldest son as heir in favour of a second son with Stewart blood probably provided the animus which sustained the intense mutual dislike between Ruairidh Macleod of Lewis and Torcail Conanach, his firstborn son from his first Mackenzie wife.

Three Torcails

Despite Ruairidh's marriage to a Stewart, a period of prolonged rebellion ensued, not only around the time of Dòmhnall Dubh's final rebellion (1545-6) but in much of the following decade. Despite this the Queen, Mary, took an interest in Torcail 'oighre' Macleod's marriage in 1563, stating that he was not to marry without her consent as he was of royal Stewart blood.[21] Unfortunately Torcail Oighre drowned in 1566 without having married or produced an heir. The subsequent lethal dynastic struggles between competing factions fatally weakened the Macleods of Lewis, cancelling their ability to present a united front to the outside world.[22] The other party between 1566 and 1574 focused on Dòmhnall Gorm of Sleat (backed by Campbell of Argyll) who had an interest in the Sìol Torcail inheritance through his connection on his mother's side (see family tree). While the Macdonalds of Sleat retained a diminishing interest thereafter, the most important of these contenders (1574-1598) were Torcail Conanach (Ruairidh's eldest son), the Mackenzie-raised and backed pretender to the chiefship (with support from the Gordon Earl of Huntly) and the third and youngest Torcail, Torcail Dubh. Barbara Stewart (Ruairidh's second wife) was still living and calling herself 'Lady Lewis' in 1568, although she must have died shortly after that. Old Ruairidh Macleod of Lewis must have loathed Torcail Conanach, and was determined not to see him succeed to his patrimony. At some time in the 1570s, Ruairidh surprised everybody (not least the pretenders to his succession) by marrying a daughter of MacLean of Duart and begetting a further two legitimate sons, the eldest of whom, Torcail Dubh, he favoured as heir, again throwing off Torcail Conanach's right to succeed as heir of Lewis. By doing so, Ruairidh effectively thwarted both Mackenzie (with Gordon-Huntly backing) and Macdonald of Sleat (Campbell-Argyll backed) attempts to secure the future direction of the Lewis inheritance.[23]

---

parosch is wastit be Lewis men.' J. Kirk, ed., The Books of Assumption of the thirds of benefices: Scottish Ecclesiastical Rentals at the Reformation (Oxford, 1995) 666-7.

21 Letter, Queen Mary to Torcail Macleod of Lewis, 1563. A facsimile and transcript of this letter in W. Fraser, ed., The Earls of Cromartie (Edinburgh, 1876) i, p. xxxiv.; Mackenzie, *History of the Outer Hebrides, 149. Argyll Transcripts, vi,* 16; 'Torqll Yre,' in *Highland Papers* ii, 50.

22 This seemed to one of the ways in which neighbours of the Macleods in the Highlands viewed the matter. A. MacCoinnich, 'Mar Phòr san t-Uisge: Ìomhaigh Sìol Torcail an Eachdraidh,' (214-231) in M. Byrne, T. O. Clancy & S. Kidd, eds., *Litreachas & Eachdraidh: Rannsachadh na Gàidhlig 2, Glaschu 2002* (Oilthigh Ghlaschu, 2006) 222.

23 *TA xii*, 129; Mackenzie, *History of the Outer Hebrides*, 150.

This ushered in a forty year period of intermittent hostility. Ruairidh's sons jockeyed for position, the disquiet focused on and fomented by Torcail Conanach with the fulsome backing of the Mackenzies, who were inexorably tightening their grip on the western seaboard in the final quarter of the sixteenth century. From the Mackenzie point of view not only was this treatment of their kinsman an affront to him but to them as well. The fact that continued support for Torcail Conanach's claims sat well with strategic Mackenzie aims was all to the good. In the immediate years following 1566, Ruairidh of Lewis was in turn captured by Torcail Conanach, released, and then forced to acknowledge Torcail Conanach as his heir (hence the sasine of 1572 discussed below in the next section). Ruairidh subsequently repudiated Torcail once he regained his freedom. This sasine was part of an attempt at papering over the cracks in the fractured relationship between Ruairidh and his estranged son Torcail Conanach. Unfortunately it failed, for Ruairidh never had any intention of favouring Torcail Conanach, preferring instead, it would seem, Torcail Dubh and Tormod, his legitimate sons from his third marriage.[24]

The Wars of the 'bastards'

To further complicate matters, there is evidence that there was an increased fishing effort from the burghs of south eastern Scotland in the Minch area at this time. These merchants and fishermen from the lowlands were, increasingly, from the 1570s onwards, coming into conflict with the islanders who wanted payments of shore dues (to which they were entitled) from them, an exaction resented by the lowlanders who complained that these rates were too high.[25] Tensions probably escalated due to the islanders' tendency to take matters into their own hands, lacking faith in the burgh courts, and providing further cause for complaint to the lowland burgesses and fishers. The burgesses and merchants of the lowlands were by no means the only interested outside parties in the lordship of the Macleods of Lewis. A glance at the family tree (Appendix C) shows the linkages of the family with the Macdonalds of Sleat in the early part of the sixteenth century and an increasingly important and not always welcome link with the Mackenzies. The Mackenzie backed heir, Torcail Conanach, kept up the pressure, and, with Mackenzie support was able to occupy Còigeach.

24 A legal deed of 1566 claiming that Ruairidh was not the father of Torcail was almost certainly a crude smear by Donald Gorm of Sleat (Argyll's candidate) to press his own right to inherit Lewis as heir to Ruairidh Macleod and an attempt at undermining Torcail 'Conanach' Mackenzie's (Huntly's candidate) claim. The presence of Bishop Carswell, Argyll's man on the witness list suggests that this scheme of 1566 had the Earl of Argyll's fingerprints all over it. When Ruairidh complained in 1574 that Torcail had kidnapped him Ruairidh repudiated Torcail's claim citing force and violence but did not deny paternity. J.R.N. MacPhail, ed., *Highland Papers, vol. ii* (Scottish History Society, Edinburgh, 1916) 280-2. Mackenzie, *History of the Outer Hebrides*, 152-3.

25 A. MacCoinnich, 'His Spirit was Given Only to Warre:' Conflict and Identity in the Scottish Gaidhealtachd c. 1580-c.1630' (133-161) in S. Murdoch & A. Mackillop eds., *Fighting for Identity. Scottish Military Experience, c.1550-1900* (Leiden, 2002) 143-5.

The Mackenzies themselves obtained a superiority over Assynt in 1592 (trouble between the Macleods and the Mackenzies in Assynt was to flare up periodically until the 1670s), consolidating their stranglehold on the Macleods' mainland possessions. Pressure piled on from the outside accentuated the cracks within Sìol Torcail. The wider Macleod kindred, Ruairidh of Lewis's five illegitimate sons among them, were forced to take different sides in a prolonged bitter and bloody struggle. The story was told from a hostile pro-Mackenzie point of view in clan histories such as that ascribed to Iain Molach (alias John Mackenzie of Applecross, c.1660) and a history by George Mackenzie the first Earl of Cromartie who labelled internecine Sìol Torcail conflict as the wars of the 'bastards.'[26]

Forfeiture and Plantation

By 1596-8, hostility between the Mackenzie backed Torcail Conanach on the one hand and Torcail Dubh Macleod of Lewis on the other reached a state of what amounted to sporadic open warfare with vicious mutual raiding. Torcail Dubh was captured and betrayed by the Brieve (hereditary judge of Lewis) and his followers and handed over to Coinneach Òg, the chief of the Mackenzies in 1598. Coinneach Òg attempted to solve the problem by summarily beheading Torcail Dubh. However, pressure had been mounting in the south for a solution to this conflict, accompanied by a ratcheting up of anti-islander rhetoric, the chorus led by James VI and orchestrated by the burghs.[27] Not only were these lands in the hands of barbarians who defied the edicts of their monarch, more importantly these same barbarians placed an impediment on the trade of 'civilised' burgesses and merchants from Lowland Scotland in the Isles. From barbarism, it was a short step to being outside the protection of the law, which in turn made the step of legally stripping the land from the Macleods that much easier.[28] Furthermore, this unrest expedited James VI's expropriation of the Macleod of Lewis lands in 1598 (planned perhaps from around 1590) and his granting of them to a consortium of nobles and burgesses from the south and east of Scotland, known as the 'Fife adventurers.' Both the king and the planters or settlers from the south hoped to gain from Lewis in different ways, the king

---

26 George Mackenzie (the first Earl of Cromartie & Lord Macleod, 1630-1740), a grandson of Torcail Conanach's daughter Mairead) and his family assumed the arms of the Macleods of Lewis, was insistent on the status of these various other Macleods as 'bastards,' with 'dissolute adherents.' No less than 4 usages of this word occur in half of one page – thus emphasising his own families right to replace them. 'History of the Family of Mackenzie' by Sir George Mackenzie, First Earl of Cromartie (pp. 462-513) in W. Fraser, ed., *The Earls of Cromartie* (Edinburgh, 1876) ii, 513. cf. J.R.N. MacPhail, ed., *Highland Papers ii*, 57, 62. For a more critical view of the Mackenzies see the same volume, the 'Ewill Trowbles of the Lewes' at p. 269-70, 276-9. MacCoinnich, 'Mar Phòr san t-Uisge,' 223-4.

27 MacCoinnich, 'Mar Phòr san t-Uisge,' 217-9.

28 A.H. Williamson, 'Scots, Indians and Empire: The Scottish Politics of Civilisation 1519-1609' (46- 83) in *Past & Present: A Journal of Historical Studies*, no. 150, 1996. p. 57-65.

by extending his control and maximising his revenues, and the new settlers by more fully exploiting the riches of the surrounding seas from their new colony in Stornoway.[29]

Opposition to Plantation

For the remaining Macleods of Lewis and many of the other clans in the north-west seaboard this was the thin end of the wedge, the colonists had a clear agenda of monopolisation of the islands resources to the exclusion of the prior inhabitants.[30] What was enacted in Lewis could well be replicated in Dunvegan, Sleat, Clanranald or Macneil lands. Even the habitually pro-crown Mackenzies saw their own interest undermined by the establishment of a new colony in the region. All these clans at various times either covertly or overtly joined factions of the Macleods of Lewis in successfully opposing this lowland settlement. This was despite three serious sustained attempts at 'planting' a colony (1598-1607), something that caused James VI & I a great deal of embarrassment.[31] Although elements of Sìol Torcail successfully saw off the attempt at colonisation the survivors were, after 10 years of sporadic conflict, no match for the Mackenzies who bought out the settlers' rights and mopped up lingering resistance from Sìol Torcail, 1609-13, securing the lands of Sìol Torcail, in the words of a contemporary their 'long wished for and expected prey.'[32]

The Aftermath

Discussion of the settlement of the Highland 'Problem' usually focuses on the Statutes of Iona (1609), a discrete set of measures taken by the government to address disorder in the region on the initiative of James VI and his bishop in the Isles, Andrew Knox. This however, arguably, was the mature expression of an ongoing initiative from the centre which had its immediate genesis in the Band of 1587 and echoes, to some extent in a much more developed form, the initiatives taken by the king's grandfather and great grandfather.[33] While

29 *CSP Scotland*, x, 331-2. M. Lynch, 'James VI and the Highland Problem' (208-227) in J. Goodare & M. Lynch, eds., *The Reign of James VI* (East Linton, 2000) 217-9 223-5. J. Goodare, *The Government of Scotland*, 1560-1625 (Oxford, 2004) 225-6.

30 *RPCS v*, 467-8; *RPCS, xiv*, Appendix to Introduction, pp. cxxviii-cxxix, *APS iv*, 160-164.

31 *CSP Scotland, xiii*, 1026; Goodare, *The Government of Scotland*, 228-9.

32 'Ewill Trowbles of the Lewes,' in MacPhail, ed., *Highland Papers ii*, p. 277; Lynch, 'James VI and the Highland Problem' p. 217-9, 223-5. MacCoinnich, 'Mar Phòr san t-Uisge,' 221.

33 M. MacGregor, 'The Statutes of Iona: Text and Context' (111-81) in *The Innes Review 57*, Autumn 2006. A.I. Macinnes, 'Crown, Clans and Fine: the 'Civilizing' of Scottish Gaeldom, 1587-1638,' (31-55) in *Northern Scotland 13*, 1993, at p. 32; J. Cameron, *James V*, 228-248. N. MacDougall, *James IV* (Edinburgh, 1997) 174-190. Julian Goodare, however, was dismissive of the Stewart monarchs' seriousness regarding the Highlands pre 1587, and views the band of 1587 as a new departure. J. Goodare, *State and Society in Early Modern Scotland* (Oxford, 1999) 254-266.

the Statutes of Iona rightly take great importance as an expression of Crown intent vis-à-vis the Highlands and Islands, there is little in them with which James V would have disagreed had such a list been seen by him some seventy years earlier. What had changed to allow James VI to succeed where others had failed? The plantation of Lewis was a self-financing project – a policy driven from the south, meant to impose 'civility' on 'barbaric' parts of the kingdom initially by a Scottish king with limited means, and latterly (1603-) by a British monarch having wider resources at his disposal. Despite this, and much to his chagrin, James VI's new initiative, a policy of plantation, failed abjectly in the northern Hebrides. The Statutes of Iona came at a time when it was realised that this new policy of plantation was unworkable in the isles. (In some senses the attempted plantation in Lewis was an attempt to extend and enforce a Lowland burghal monopoly over an entire region that was disadvantaged by this.) The Statutes coincided with the relinquishing of the planters' rights in Lewis over to the Mackenzies, a process endorsed by the Crown in 1609 and achieved by Mackenzies two years later. The Mackenzies who controlled the adjacent coasts on Ross-shire, and had been amassing pieces of Sìol Torcail territory piecemeal since 1588, succeeded where lowland burgesses at the end of a long supply chain from Fife had failed.[34] A national Scottish, and even 'British' after 1603, initiative had failed. The centre's Highland 'problem' was ultimately only resolved with a solution that was at least partly 'local.'

The New Order

It might be helpful too to view the Statutes of Iona as one part of James VI's settlement of the Highlands and Islands, rather than as an end in itself. Why would chiefs who had regularly cocked a snook at Edinburgh, now meekly accept such terms as offered by James? One reason was an increased English naval presence, which combined with Campbell hegemony south of Ardnamurchan meant that James had more leverage than his predecessors. This was a British rather than a Scottish monarch. North of Ardnamurchan and in the North Minch, Jacobean policy and intentions were not implemented by the Statutes but by the regional dominance of the Mackenzies. They assumed control (either directly or by proxy) of all of the former Sìol Torcail territory in the North Minch basin (save Eddrachilles). In addition to this the Mackenzies became virtual viceroys in the North Minch region.[35]

---

34 Cailean Cam (d.1594), chief of the Mackenzies had obtained the superiority of Assynt in 1588. MacCoinnich, *Tùs gu Iarlachd ii*, PT. 2.4, P.T 2.7, tdd. 417, 447, 450, 455. The burgh of Aberdeen gave help to "puir men that com fra the Lewis, for thair support..' and towards the '...support of sex cost syd men that wer pilleit be the Hileand men, in thair cumming fra the Lewis...' in early 1599 in: J.Stuart, ed., *Extracts from the Council Register of the burgh of Aberdeen Vol. 2, 1570-1625* (Aberdeen Spalding Club, 1848) 71, 204. Thanks to Dr Dauvit Horsbroch for this last reference.

35 MacCoinnich, 'His Spirit was Given only to Warre,' 148-9; MacCoinnich, *Tùs gu Iarlachd* Caib.4.34, tdd. 228-230.

A case in point was Tròndarnais (Trotternish), in north Skye. This had been a disputed territory for much of the sixteenth century with control over it hotly contested by Sìol Torcail, the Macleods of Harris (Sìol Tormoid) and the Macdonalds of Sleat. The fighting between Sìol Tormoid and Sliochd Uisdein (the Macdonalds of Sleat) over these lands reached its nadir in and around 1601.[36] This dispute was only finally resolved under the overlordship of the Mackenzies, whose strength in the area, backed when necessary, presumably, with English naval support, made both Sìol Tormoid and Macdonal pretensions untenable. Coinneach Òg Mackenzie of Kintail having taken control of the former Sìol Torcail lands, including Bhatarnais (Vaternish) before 1607, sold Bhatarnais to Ruairidh Mòr MacLeòid of Dunvegan who in return gave up his claim on Tròndarnais to Mackenzie.[37] Mackenzie then granted Tròndarnais to Macdonald of Sleat as his vassal (tenant) for these lands. Ruairidh Mòr MacLeòid of Harris died and was buried in Chanonry, attending the seat of the Mackenzies, who numbered MacNeil of Barra and Clanranald as their 'vassals' together with Sleat for some if not all of their possessions. (The Mackenzies also shielded the MacLeans of Duart from debt in this period.) Sìol Torcail were all but eradicated, the exceptions being the Macleods of Assynt and Coigeach, vassals of the Mackenzies since the 1590s, and Sliochd MhicGhillechaluim or the Macleods of Raasay, vassals to the Mackenzies from 1608. The role of the Mackenzies in crown policy is further underlined by the assent of Andrew Knox, bishop of the Isles, to the transfer of the superiority of Raasay from the bishopric over to Coinneach Òg Mackenzie of Kintail on New Year's Day 1608.[38]

---

36 A. Nicholson, *History of Skye* (2nd ed., Ard Bhearnasdail, 1994) 23, 28-9, 32-4, 47, 49, 63-70. MacGregor, 'The Statutes of Iona: Text and Context,' 133-6.

37 *RPCS xiv*, 539; R.C. Macleod, ed., *The Book Of Dunvegan, Being documents from the muniments room of the Macleods..., Vol. 1, 1340-1700* (Aberdeen, 1938) p. 78-81.

38 MacCoinnich, *Tùs gu Iarlachd*, Caib 4.34, tdd. 228-334; 422-4. The Mackenzies assumed overlordship of Raasay in 1608, and became feudal superiors of the MacGilleChallums of Raasay thereafter. Mackenzie stipulated that galley service was due to him from MacGillechalum whenever he required it together with a rental payment. This and a note of a charter to MacDonald of Sleat by Kenneth (Coinneach Òg) Mackenzie, Lord Kintail (†1611) of the lands of Trotternish, renewed by Colin Mackenzie, Lord Kintail in 1622. (copy, 1873, of original documents) *NAS GD 128/23/ (Bundle)* 2; "Inventory of the Writtis and evidentis delyverit be Alex[ande]r Mc Gillichallum of Rasay To ane Nobill Lord Coline earle of Seafort upone the 27th day of April 1629 yeirs.' Charter by Bishop Knox confirmed 27 April 1609. *RMS vii*, no. 298, p. 110-112; cf. *NAS RS 37/1 fol. 19; NAS RS 37/5 fol. 32v. NAS GD 305/1/166/7*

II

While one could think of things purely in terms of the dynastic and political, I would like to briefly consider the wider human and geographic aspects of the Lordship in this section. The geographical implications of this are more apparent when one considers a map. This shows us that the Macleods of Lewis could control the entire North Minch basin from their bases on the mainland, Raasay, Bhatarnais, and Lewis. The importance of seagoing links is clear, and frequent transport back and forth was an essential feature of this lordship. This had obvious dangers, and indeed one of the many turning points in the family history of the period was the unfortunate death of Torcail Oighre in 1566 (discussed above), when in cross-channel transit between various parts of the Sìol Torcail Lordship, he and 60 of his followers were caught in a storm off the coast of Trotternish and all were lost.[39]

An Tìr & na Daoine

Sìol Torcail were proprietors of land not only in Lewis, but in Asaint, Còigeach and Bhatarnais. They also effectively held Raasay 'by the sword' from the Bishop of the Isles, i.e. the bishop could not evict them (or probably collect rent), it was thought in 1549, even though he was titular landlord.[40] There were also elements of Sìol Torcail in Eddrachilles, and they continued to occupy part of Gairloch without title (until around 1611) despite the overlordship and pressure here from the Mackenzies from 1494 onwards.[41] The nature of the make up of Sìol

39 Mackenzie, *History of the Outer Hebrides,* 149. This was paralleled around 100 years later when Macleod of Raasay, attended his superior, Mackenzie of Seaforth (whose line supplanted the Macleods of Lewis) in Lewis and was also lost at sea. 'Marbhrann do Iain MacGilleChaluim Ratharsaidh' (c.1671) J. Carmichael Watson, *Gaelic Songs of Mary Macleod* (SGTS, Edinburgh, 1934) 26-8; 114-5. A contemporary account of this is offered in W. Mackay ed., *Chronicles of the Frasers. The Wardlaw Manuscript Entitled 'Polichrinicon Seu Policratica Temporum, Or, The True Genealogy of the Fraser, 916-1674, by Master James Fraser* (Edinburgh, 1905) 498-9. Thanks to Dr Michel Byrne for this last reference.

40 ('Malcolm' seems to have been the Scots/English form used for the personal name 'Gillechallum.') A Malcolm MacGillechalum obtained a grant to Raasay, formerly technically the property of the Bishop of the Isles, from James VI in 1596. The Mackenzies assumed overlordship of Raasay in 1608, and became feudal superiors of the MacGilleChallums of Raasay thereafter. Mackenzie stipulated that galley service was due to him from MacGillechalum whenever he required it together with a rental payment. *NAS GD 128/23/ (Bundle) 2*; "Inventory of the Writtis and evidentis delyverit be Alex[ande]r Mc Gillichallum of Rasay To ane Nobill Lord Coline earle of Seafort upone the 27th day of April 1629 yeirs.' (This a copy of the original document made in 1873.) My thanks to Dr Alasdair Ross, for this reference.

41 'The McLeods lairds of Lews were possesd of a large Estate viz., The Sixteen davochs of the Lews now possesed by my Lord Seafort, The Four Davochs of Watterniss, now possesed by the laird of McLeod the four Davochs of Rasay now possesed by Macleod of Raasay, the foure davoch of Coigach possesed be the Earl of Cromarty the four davoch of Gairloch now possesed by Mackenzie of Garloch the four davoch of Assint now possesed by Mackenzie of Assint and the four davoch of Eddarachilles by the Lord Reay being in all fourty davoch of land.' In, 'The

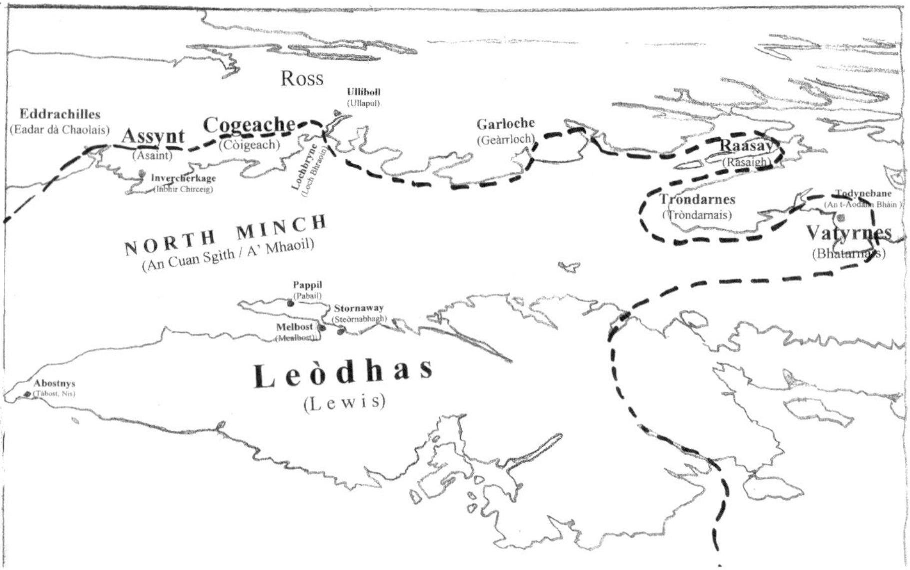

Torcail in terms of the personnel in their lordship is best demonstrated by the witness list to a hitherto overlooked sasine (transfer of land) following a grant of land to Torcail Conanach Macleod, as son and heir of his father in 1572.

The ceremony was carried out at the four parts of the Macleod lordship on successive days, at Ullapool for Còigeach, at Inverkirkaig for Assynt, at Bayble (Pabail) for Lewis, and at Todynebane (An t-Aodann Bhàin/Edinbane) for Vaternish, 5-21 April 1572. This witness list reads as follows:

> 'Donaldo mcGillecallum Wore in Raisey; Donaldo mcAne Duemoyr in Garloche; Johanne mcConnill mcAne mcMurche in Lochbryne; Donald mcThomas Due in Lochbrehim; Ewyr mcConnyll mcKennych moyr in LochBreyn; Donaldo mcThomas dhu in Loch Breyn; Allano filio A[n]gusi bref in Abost Nyss in Lewis; John Gor filio Willelmi mcGillepadrik mcBref in Lewis; Angusio mcW[illia]m mcGillePadrik mcBref in Le[wis]; Gillepadrik mcAne mcIllepadrik in Melbost in Lewis; Roderic mcAne wcConyll wcThomas in Lewis; Johanno filio Angus Denowne; Johanno dow Frass[e]r; Johanno roy [mcRore] mcLachlayne McOler; Murdo mcRorie mcLachlayne; Donaldo mcAne mcFarchyr mcAneglas; Johanno Glas mcAne mcKanyche eyre, familio Torquili Makkloid; Wyllelmo mcJethe(?) row(?) in Lochbryme; Alex[andr]o mcDonald wcAnedue

---

Genealogy of the family of Assint' (1739) *NLS MS 19308* fol. 4. For a discussion, of 'davochs,' a unit of land, see A. Ross, 'The Dabhach in Moray: a new look at an old tub'. pp. 57-74, In A. Woolf, ed., *Landscape and Environment in Dark Age Scotland. St John's House Papers, 11* (St Andrews University, 2006).

ibidem; Thormat Coyr mcAne [mcHee?] in Pappall in Lewis; Gillecallum mcNeyl wcFarcher ibidem; Allano mc Gillechallum mc [Thormac McAnedue?] ibidem; Thormat mcAne due ibidem; Johanno McThormat [mcAnedue ibidem]; Allexandro mcConyll Galliche in [Caithness(?)]; Angusi [mcMurche] mcConyll in Lewis; [Kenneth McAne McGechyn, servitor Torquili Makkloid?][42] (See appendix B)

This is effectively a list of the leading men in the Macleod lordship in 1572, some of whom are unattested (as far as I know) in any other surviving document. Some of these are readily identifiable, such as the men of Gairloch and Raasay.[43] However Donald, the son of Gille Chaluim mòr (alias Malcolm) the first of Raasay has hitherto been unknown to genealogists and we are offered an intriguing glimpse of some others such as the mens' names here from Loch Broom and some of the patronymics of the Lewis witnesses at Pabail.[44] Two of the groups of witnesses, however, are known (if imprecisely) to tradition and to history – Clann mhic Amhlaigh (Macaulays) of Uig in Lewis, and Sliochd a' Bhreitheimh, the brieves or hereditary judges (later known as Morrisons) traditionally associated with Ness in Lewis, but probably operating more widely within the Macleod lordship. However this, 'Allano filio A[n]gusi bref in Abost Nyss in Lewis,' clearly offers documentary evidence corroborating oral tradition which associated the brieves or hereditary judges with Tàbost, Nis (Habost, Ness).[45]

---

42 I footnoted this in an earlier article but have revisited this document since then. MacCoinnich, 'Mar Phòr san t-Uisge' (2002) 214. This document, *NAS RH 6/2247*, is in Latin, but the names in the witness list alternate between Latinate and Scotticised forms of Gaelic names. For an attempt at interpreting these names in their Gaelic context see appendix B. I have amended the reading following consultation of the document. I have left the names I was unable to read from the document in square brackets and followed the reading provided by the calendar in the NAS. *Calendar of Charters and other original documents preserved in H.M. General Register House., Vol. X, No. 2247.* N.B. 'C'and 'T' are notoriously difficult to differentiate in manuscript hands of this period. I have decided, with reservations on a reading of 'Thormot' rather than 'Chormac' as the former (Tormod / Norman) is well attested in Lewis and the latter name is very rare. The 'h' in Tormod is possibly there by analogy with the form 'Thomas.' I am grateful to Professor Thomas Clancy for this suggestion.

43 'Donaldo mcAne Duemoyr in Garloche' = Dòmhnall mac Iain Duibh mòr an Geàrrloch ? For a traditional tale of a crime commited by a 'mac Iain Duibh' from Gairloch see J.H. Dixon, Gairloch and a Guide to Loch Maree (Edinburgh, 1886: Reprinted 1974) 44.

44 Morrison, *The Macleods - The Genealogy of a Clan*, iv, p. 32-5. The name 'Iwer' (Ìomhair mac Dhòmhnaill mhic Choinnich mhòir) despite the patronymic suggests that this person was connected in some way to the 'Macivers' of Loch Broom (Inverlael), relatively well attested in charters of the time. cf. 'Innes McEwer' (1614, 1635) *RPCS x*, 256, 259; T. Thomson ed., *Inquisitionum ad Capellam Domini Regis Retornatam quae in Publicus Archiivs Scotiae adhuc servantur abbreviato* (3 Vols., Edinburgh, 1811-16) ii, 83. Both a John Maciver, 'officaur of Lochbrume,' and the 'Donald mcAne Dow' named in the sasine above appear in a surviving Mackenzie account from 1569. 'And wt thrie scoir xiii li[bres] v S iii d rasavit fra Jhon McEvir in name of Donald m^cAne Dow the ix day of Februar in p[ar]t of paiment of the thua p[ar]t of the p[ar]sonage & vicarage of Loc[h] Brume crope I^m sextie nyne.' MacCoinnich, *Tùs gu Iarlachd*, ii, 381, 384.

45 This document was unknown to William Matheson, who reconstructed the Genealogy of the

Macaulays of Lewis

Those named here as 'Mac Oler' are probably better recognised as MacAmhlaigh or Macaulay traditionally identified as belonging to Uig. Tales collected by Captain Thomas in the nineteenth century identified an Iain Ruadh Macaulay, the grandfather of Donald Cam MacAmhlaigh, who it was thought (then) flourished in the fifteenth century.[46] Dòmhnall Cam, however, is actually on record in 1610, and if Iain Ruadh really was his grandfather as tradition had it, a date in the mid sixteenth rather than the fifteenth century might seem reasonable. If the name listed in the sasine as 'mc Oler' is MacAmhlaigh then this is possibly the 'John Roy Macaulay' of these tales, with a slightly different genealogy to that given by Thomas from tradition.[47] Thomas struggled to connect these persons to earlier history or traditions of 'Macaulays' within Lewis, he did notice that there were traditions linking the Macaulays with Wester Ross, and Loch Broom probably in the fifteenth century or earlier.[48] While tradition may well have forgotten any direct link, the context of a wider Macleod, trans-Minch lordship provides a clear set of circumstances linking branches of this kin on both sides of the Minch.

The Lordship

While historical sources can give us the occasional glimpse of some of the personnel, they can also give us some, limited, information about the landscape they inhabited between 1500 and 1610. A brief list can give a flavour of this: the castle at Stornoway, Macleod's orchard at Eilean Chaluim Cille (Lochs), the 3000 salmon taken in Barvas in 1585, the annual harvest of 'colkis' ('guga' or juvenile gannet) on Sula Sgeir by Niseachs (Nessmen, north Lewis), the 'wild' sheep of the Flannans which Macleod's tenants 'hunted,' and Ruairidh

'Morrisons' in 1977. W. Matheson, 'The Morrisons of Ness' in *TGSI 50*, 1976-8, 60-80; W. Matheson, ed, *The Blind Harper/An Clàrsair Dall* (Edinburgh, 1970) 186-9. See also my brief piece 'Dùn Èistean and the Morrisons: The Historical Background' in *Criomagan* (Comann Eachdraidh Nis) àir. 38, Dùbhlachd 2006, t.d. 8-10.

46 Probably John Roy (son of Roderick and grandson of Lachlan) Macaulay and his brother, Murdo, in this document in 1573 rather than John Roy and his brother Malcolm sometime in the 1450s as given by tradition. F.W.L. Thomas, 'Traditions of the Macaulays of Lewis' *PSAS 14* (1879-80) 387-98.

47 'Donald Cam McCoull and Mulcallum McCoull,' 1610. *RPCS ix*, 16, 19; 'mctowell John og mctowell all bretheren sick mc towell, Donald mctowll and thair haill childrene, tenentis...' Notice of intention to evict the tenants of Uig, Lewis, 1605. The 't' is probably a mistranscription of the 'c,' thus this surname should read 'McCowl' (i.e. MacAmhlaigh / Macaulay). This, R.C. Macleod, ed., *The Book Of Dunvegan, Being documents from the muniments room of the Macleods, Vol. 1, 1340-1700* (Aberdeen, 1938) p 116.

48 Thomas, 'Traditions of the Macaulays,' 370, 384, 388. 'History of the Family of Mackenzie' by Sir George Mackenzie, First Earl of Cromartie (462-513) in W. Fraser, ed., *The Earls of Cromartie* (Edinburgh, 1876) ii, 466-8. 'Geanalogie of the Surname of Mackenzie' in MacPhail ed., Highland *Papers ii*, 15-17.

Macleod's retreat at Pabaidh in Loch Roag, Lewis, which he retired to when he was 'feirit' (frightened). Information such as this, although still sparse in detail, provides some indication of the centres of activity.[49] The archaeological record may in the future augment such information with fresh evidence on which the written record is silent.[50] Another indicator of the size, and potential power of Sìol Torcail is provided by estimates of the manpower available to them around this time compiled by English intelligence, nervous about 'Redshank' activity in the Irish wars of the 1590s. Lewis, it was thought, could provide 700 fighting men for Macleod (not counting those obliged to remain at home and look after the crops and livestock), Bernera in Lewis 60 men, Vaternish would raise 200 men for Macleod of Lewis, and a further 80 men from Raasay. This comes to a total of 1040 men and, as the compiler of the list concentrated on islands, the territories of Eadar dà Chaolais, Asaint, Còigeach and Geàrrloch were not included. If those areas were added, the manpower available to Macleod may well have come to over 1300.[51] While these figures might not seem particularly large to us, it is worth remembering that the estimated population of Scotland was far smaller than it is today – probably around 20% of current rates.[52]

49 For these and for further information see: the volumes of the *Register of the Privy Council of Scotland* (especially 1598-1615); an anonymous description of the Lewis from about 1570-90 printed in Skene's *Celtic Scotland* (Edinburgh, 1880) vol. iii, p. 428-30); J.R.N. MacPhail, ed., *Highland Papers* (Edinburgh, 1916) ii, 265-288. R.W. Munro, ed., Donald Monro's 'Description of the Occidental i.e. Western Islands of Scotland who travelled through many of them Anno 1549' (included, pp. 287-346) in M. Martin, *A Description of the Western Islands of Scotland circa 1695* (Birlinn edition, Edinburgh, 1999) 320-323, 333-9. 183-5. A. Mitchell, ed., *Geographical Collections Relating to Scotland made by Walter Macfarlane* (Edinburgh, 1907) ii, 183-5.

50 Investigations are currently being conducted by archaeologists Rachel Barrowman and Chris Barrowman (GUARD) of the University of Glasgow at Dùn Èistean, traditionally the stronghold of Sliochd a' Bhreitheamh (Clann MhicGilleMhoire) in Ness in north Lewis. See their website, **http://www.duneistean.org/index.php** (accessed, 23 August 2007).

51 W.F. Skene, ed., *Celtic Scotland* (Edinburgh, 1880) iii, 438-433; The lands of the neighbouring Macdonalds of Sleat (Slèite, 700; Tròndairnis, 600; and Uibhist a Tuath, 300), by way of comparison would raise 1600 men. Macleod of Harris (Dunvegan) could, not counting his mainland possession of Gleann Eilg, raise a total of 680 men (Na Hearadh,140; Pabaigh, 40; Diùirinis, Bracadail and Minginis 500). For reports of the Macleods of Lewis and other islanders in Ireland in July-August 1595 see CSP Scot xi, 253-5, 629, 637-8, 677, 684-5, 687-8. J. O' Donovan ed., *Annala Rioghachta Eireann: Annals of the Kingdom of Ireland by the Four Masters* (Dublin, 1851) vi, p. 1974-1975.

52 Captain Dymes estimated the population of Lewis in total to be around 4000 in 1630. Mackenzie, History of the Outer Hebrides (1903 edition) Appendix F, p. 592-3. (The 2001 census numbered 19,918 people on Lewis and Harris. GRO, Scotland.) The population of Scotland as a whole is estimated at one million in 1690. T.C. Smout, A History of the Scottish People, 1560-1830 (Glasgow, 1969) 111. R.A. Houston & I.D. Whyte, eds., Scottish Society, 1500-1800 (Cambridge, 1989) 3. The General Register Office, Scotland state that the population of Scotland in June 2006 was 5,116, 900. <http://www.gro-scotland.gov.uk/> (accessed 28 August 2007).

III

Having briefly considered the dynastic and political history and then wider aspects of the human and geographic shape of the lordship of the Macleods of Lewis in the first two parts of this paper, I would like in the final part, to consider some of the wider issues germane to the points raised in the first two sections.

The North Minch Fishery

An early seventeenth century account – albeit for the purpose of raising capital for a fishery company – described the Minch as one of the richest fisheries in Europe. Even allowing for a little exaggeration this description was probably not too far off the mark.[53] This cross-Minch landholding meant that Sìol Torcail effectively controlled the shores of the entire North Minch basin and the resources in and around this area. A glance at a map of the north Minch basin (above) also makes sense of the Fife Adventurers' desire to secure a harbour at Stornoway (1598-1609). For the settlers, the opportunity to properly exploit the fisheries with a secure base, and thus not be prey to the exactions of highland landlords, must have been a liberating prospect. Despite the fact that landlords such as the Macleods and others were within their legal rights to exact ground dues from fishermen who came ashore to preserve their catch and fix their equipment, it was a form of taxation which the merchant-fishermen hated paying, frequently complaining that they were being overcharged, and when they refused to pay the Macleods seemingly were not slow to 'bill and straik' lowland merchants and fishermen.[54]

Steve Boardman's research has uncovered the importance of the fisheries as an economic underpinning of Campbell lordship in Argyll in the fifteenth and sixteenth centuries. Despite their political connections at the highest levels even the Campbells experienced difficulty in developing their trade due to burghal opposition and intransigence.[55] Research on the Mackenzies who took

53 *NAS GD 46/20/Box 5; NAS GD46/18/139; NAS GD46/18/147.* A. MacCoinnich, 'Native, Stranger and the Fishing of the Isles, 1611-1637,' in A.I. Macinnes, L. Francois & S. Murdoch eds., *Pirates, Capitalists and Imperialists from North Sea and Baltic States, c.1400-1945* (NEHRN Proceedings, vol. 2, forthcoming).

54 '…being greatlie offendit wt the many injures and oppressiones that wer done to ther freindis and to fischermen on the cost syd that yeirlie repairit unto the fisching of the Lewes, be the men of the Lewes in spoiling tham & taking ther barkes & straking and billing [assaulting] some of them, they complain to his Majestie of these wrongis...' Account of chaplain to Fife Adventurers, *NLS Wod. Qu. Vol. XX.*, fol. 352-357v; MacCoinnich, *Tùs gu Iarlachd*, PT. 2.7, td. 446. MacCoinnich, 'His Spirit Was Given to Warre,' 144-6.

55 Steve Boardman suggested that dissatisfaction over fishery policy may have induced Colin, Earl of Argyll to rebell in 1488. S. Boardman, 'Pillars of the Community: Campbell Lordship and Architectural Patronage in the Fifteenth Century' (123-159) in R. Oram & G. Stell eds., *Lordship*

over the Sìol Torcail inheritance in the seventeenth century reveals a similar picture. They too tried to develop their fishery and were, to an extent, stymied, by burghal opposition (with the added complication of English interference) despite their political connections.[56] If even the Campbells in the fifteenth and the Mackenzies in the seventeenth centuries had their entrepreneurial designs thwarted despite their powerful political connections, then kindred such as the Macleods of Lewis or perhaps the Macdonalds had no chance of bucking the burghal monopoly. A recent article by Martin Rorke underlines the importance of the fishing industry in the West Highlands and Islands as a driver for Crown interest and burgess activity there.[57]

Archdeacon Donald Monro's itinerary (1549) in the Isles is instructive in what it does mention in relation to the sea. Almost every other entry for each island has an observation of the relative merits of fish and fishing and comments on the harbours and anchorages of many of these locations. While Monro may have been preoccupied with clerical income, one may also wonder whether this fishing wealth was potential or actually being prosecuted. If, however, rather than having a great imagination, Monro was actually recording this activity as it was in fact being prosecuted (even allowing for some exaggeration) and not appearing in the records of southern and eastern Scotland, thus not bringing any revenue to the burghs and Crown, this would also do much to explain the upsurge of crown and lowland burgh interest in the region in the latter half of the sixteenth century. This, while speculative, raises the possibility that people in the north and west Highlands were simply bypassing the jealously guarded burgh monopolies and trading with foreigners such as the Dutch who had a strong presence in the area from the 1540s and possibly earlier.[58]

Indolent Gaels?

To assume that there was no trade merely because the burghs were unable to get their hands on it and record this may well be misleading. Concomitant assumptions that Highlanders or Gaels were (and are) either not capable of

and Architecture in Medieval and Renaissance Scotland (Edinburgh, 2005) at 146-148. S. Boardman, *The Campbells, 1250-1513* (Edinburgh, 2006) 295-300, 304-5.

56 MacCoinnich, *Tùs gu Iarlachd*, 276, 298-349. A. MacCoinnich, 'Native, Stranger and the Fishing of the Isles, 1611-1637,' in A.I. Macinnes, L. Francois & S. Murdoch eds., *Pirates, Capitalists and Imperialists from North Sea and Baltic States, c.1400-1945* (NEHRN Proceedings, vol. 2: 2006, forthcoming).

57 M. Rorke, 'The Scottish Herring Trade, 1470-1600' (149-165) in the *Scottish Historical Review 84*, 2005, p. 160-165.

58 R.W. Munro, ed., Donald Monro's 'Description of the Occidental i.e. Western Islands of Scotland who travelled through many of them Anno 1549' (included, pp. 287-346) in M. Martin, *A Description of the Western Islands of Scotland circa 1695* (Birlinn edition, Edinburgh, 1999); Boardman, *The Campbells, 1250-1513*, p. 296-7. MacKenzie, *History of the Outer Hebrides*, p. 586. R.K. Hannay, & D. Hay, eds., *The Letters of James V* (Edinburgh, 1954) 408-9.

industry or disengaged with commerce, and that being barbarous and rebellious or backward was the expected state of affairs, should be challenged.[59] Despite the best intentions of historians these notions are deep-rooted and pervasive, due to the extent to which this 'official' southern-generated viewpoint dominates the source material for the period. Even the staunchly pro-island W.C. Mackenzie's *History of the Outer Hebrides*, is guilty of this to some extent due to reliance on such source material. A future research agenda should try to cast off the straitjacket imposed by 'external' sources and try to interpret, as far as is possible, the forgotten 'local' perspective as a valid alternative viewpoint. Why were the Macleods and Macdonalds rebelling for much of the sixteenth century? Rather than accepting rebellion as a 'natural' condition for people from the Highlands and Islands, more should be done to develop a local perspective – a perspective which perhaps modern historians – like the king, Crown, burghs and the Fife adventurers in the sixteenth and seventeenth centuries, have sometimes disregarded to their own loss.

59 For a discussion of these paradigms see, A. MacCoinnich, "Cleiffis of Irne': Clann Choinnich agus Gnìomhachas Iarainn, c. 1569-1630,' (137-154) in W. McLeod, J.E. Fraser & A. Gunderloch, eds., *Cànan & Cultar / Language & Culture: Rannsachadh na Gàidhlig 3* (Edinburgh, 2006) 137-8, 149. Macinnes has challenged these paradigms albeit from a different perspective, pushing the origins of a move from 'traditionalism' towards 'commercialism' back into the late seventeenth century. A.I. Macinnes, *Clanship, Commerce and the House of Stuart, 1603-1788* (East Linton, 1996) 18-19, 142-153, 172.

Conclusion

The lands of Sìol Torcail in Lewis were inextricably linked to the fate of the kindred's possessions and tenants in Skye, Raasay and the mainland, throughout the sixteenth century and beyond. The plantation centred in Lewis affected and drew a powerful reaction from the whole region. While Sìol Torcail successfully resisted the Fife Adventurers they were then unable to offer resistance to the Mackenzies. The Mackenzies were ultimately the crown's chosen method of suppressing not only the Macleods of Lewis but of imposing control on neighbouring kindreds in the whole North Minch region (1609-37), such as the Macleods of Dunvegan and the Macdonalds of Sleat. While the Crown, and their partners the burghs and merchants, chose to dress up their attempt at colonisation in Lewis (1598-1609) in the language of 'civility' and 'progress' (and they may also have believed this), it would seem reasonable to suggest that a desire to maximise their own profits from the fishing grounds might have been an equally pressing motive. In terms of Sìol Torcail, documentary historians relied on evidence, the weight of which overwhelmingly has been left to us from the enemies of the Macleods – and have mirrored the bias of the sources, considering the Macleods of Lewis (Macdonalds too) as somehow being naturally 'rebellious,' and by implication 'uncivilised.' Future research should try to do more to understand the underlying causes of these rebellions from the forgotten 'local' perspective, in as much as this is possible.[60]

60 I am grateful to my colleagues, Dr Michel Byrne and Professor Thomas O. Clancy for taking time from their busy schedules to read drafts of this paper and for making suggestions, while making clear that they are not responsible for any shortcomings in this paper.

Abbreviations

APS	*Acts of Parliaments of Scotland*, 1424-1707, T. Thomson & C. Innes, eds. (12 vols., Edinburgh, 1814-1875)
AT	*Argyll Transcripts*, made by the 10th Duke of Argyll. Photostat copies of extracts in the Department of Scottish History, University of Glasgow
BL	British Library, London
CSP Scot	*Calendar of State Papers Relating to Scotland and Mary Queen of Scots, 1547-1603*, J. Bain et al eds. (13 vols., Edinburgh,1898-1969)
ER	*The Exchequer rolls of Scotland 1264-1600: Rotuli Scaccarii Regum* Scotorum 1264-1600, G. Burnett, G. P. Mcneill eds.(Edinburgh, 23 vols, 1878-1908)
NAS	National Archives of Scotland, Edinburgh
NLS	National Library of Scotland, Edinburgh
PSAS	Proceedings of the Society of Antiquaries of Scotland
RMS	*Registrum Magni Sigilli Regum Scotorum: Register of the Great Seal of Scotland, 1306-1668*, Thomson, J.M., ed. (Edinburgh, *11 Vols, 1882-1914*: Clark Constable Reprint, 1984)
RPCS	*Register of the Privy Council of Scotland* (1545-1625) D. Masson, J. H. Burton eds. (first series, vols. 1-14, Edinburgh, 1877-1898)
RSS	*Registrum Secreti Sigilli regum Scotorum: Register of the Privy Seal of Scotland 1488-1580*, M. Livingstone et al eds. (Edinburgh, 7 vols, 1948-1966)
TA	*Accounts of the Lord High Treasurer of Scotland 1473-1580: Compota Thesaurariorum Regum Scotorum 1473-1580*, T. Dickson, J. B. Paul, & C.T. Macinnes (13 vols., Edinburgh, 1877-1978)
TGSI	Transactions of the Gaelic Society of Inverness

Appendix A – Timeline: Sìol Torcail in the Sixteenth Century	
1493	Forfeiture of Lordship of the Isles
1494	Eachann Ruadh MacCoinnich [Hector Mackenzie] gets title to Gairloch
1498	Torcail Macleod given the bailliary of Tròndarnais (& Duntulm) by James IV
1502	Torcail declared an outlaw and rebel – royal demand of 9 years back mails of Tròndarnais and custody of the person of Dòmhnall Dubh. Torcail's lands (named) of Lewis, Assynt, Coigeach and Vaterness forfeit to the king.
1506	Royal expedition against rebels of Lewis including a ship named 'the Raven' (& Crown forces possibly supported by Alasdair Crotach of Harris); Spaniards captured in Lewis.
1509	Malcolm (mac Roderick) Macleod (alias 'Gillecallum' of Rasay ?) given remission for late rebellion
1511	Malcolm (Gillecalum) Macleod, Torcail's brother, granted Lewis by James IV
1530	John (mac Torcail) Macleod, chief of Lewis summoned to Edinburgh
1533	Ruairidh (mac Malcolm) Macleod attempting to gain entry to forfeited lands of Lewis?
1536	Mr Roderick Farquharson Hectorissone presented to the churches of Barvas (Leòdhas), Kilmuir (E. Sgitheanach) and Kilchoman (Ile)
1538	Ruaraidh MacLeòid, son to the late Malcolm, finally succesful in getting control of barony of Lewis
1539-40	Rebellion, followed by Royal Expedition. Ruaraidh married Barbara Stewart, 1541
1545-6	Dòmhnall Dubh Rebellion; and, 1546-50, further sentences of forfeiture and declaration of Macleod as rebel
1549	Dean Monro's Description, Pabaigh, Eilean Chaluim Cille, Rasaigh etc.
1550	Remission to Ruairidh for rebellion, murder and non-attendance of the Queen's armies.
1555	Charges of treason raised against Ruairidh
1566	Death of Torcail Oighre precipitates succession crisis. Instrument related to Hugh the Brieve's deathbed "confession." Torcail Conanach disinherited. Torcail with Mackenzie help kidnaps Ruairidh.

Appendix A – Timeline: Sìol Torcail in the Sixteenth Century	
1571/2	Torcail Conanach recognised as heir by Ruairidh in peace deal. (Sasine) However, Ruairidh reneges, subsequently marries sister of Duart, has other legitimate sons
1576-8	Ruairidh taking Caution with the Privy Council not to interfere with fishing.
1584	Old Ruairidh Macleod of Lewis repudiates Torcail Conanach and his son John
1585	Torcail Conanach supported by the Mackenzies and the Earl of Huntly
1588-90	Reports of plan by king to forfeit Macleods and install Bothwell in Lewis. (English spies fear Spanish money will be used for this end).
1591/2	Colin (Cailean Cam) Mackenzie of Kintail secures a Crown grant of Assynt.
1593	Torcail Conanach confined to Còigeach and 'oppressed' by his 'usurping' half brother.
1595?	Death of Ruairidh; Reports of Macleods of Lewis, Harris, and Macdonalds of Sleat participating in Irish wars
1597	Torcail dubh Macleod of Lewis, raiding and wasting Còigeach and Loch Broom, held by Torcail Conanach. Capture and Execution of Torcail Dubh MacLeoid, by brieve and Mackenzie,.
1598	Expropriation of Macleods; "…that na part nor portioun of the Hielandis nor Iles, according to the Act imprentit , beiring thairin his Majesties declaratioun, salbe al be at ony tyme heirefter disponit, in few, tak or utherwayes, bot to Lawland men…"
1605	Fresh attempt at Settlement by Fife Adventurers
1609	Adventures sell up / quit - Mackenzie granted the Isle of Lewis
1611	John Mackenzie of Gairloch given commission to use fire and sword against Gairloch Macleods

Appendix B - Attempted Reconstruction of the Names in the Witness List of the Macleod Sasine, 1572, using modern Gaelic

Dòmhnall mac Gille Chaluim Mhòir ann an Rasaigh, ...(Raasay)
Dòmhnall mac Iain Dhuibh Mhòir ann an Geàrrloch........(Gairloch)
Iain mac Dhòmhnaill mhic Iain mhic Mhurchaidh ann an
Loch Bhraoin........(Loch Broom)
Dòmhnall mac Thòmais Dhuibh ann an Loch Bhraoin........(Loch Broom)
Ìomhar mac Dhòmhnaill mhic Choinnich mhòir ann an Loch Bhraoin
Dòmhnall mac Thòmais dhuibh ann an Loch Bhraoin ....(Loch Broom)
Ailean mac Aonghais a' bhreitheamh ann an Tàbost Nis
ann an Leòdhas........(Habost, Ness, Lewis)
Iain Geàrr, mac do dh'Uilleam mhic Gille Pàdraig, mac
a' bhreitheamh ann an........(Ness ? Lewis)
Gillepàdraig mac Iain Maol-Pàdraig ann am Mealbost Leòdhais........(Melbost Lewis)
Ruairidh mac Iain mhic Dhòmhnaill MhicLeòid ann an Leòdhas........(Lewis)
Iain mac Aonghais Denoun[61] ....(Lewis)
Iain Dubh Friseal........(Lewis)
Iain Ruadh mac Ruairidh mhic Laclainn MhicAmhlaigh........(Uig ?, Lewis)
Murchadh mac Ruairidh mhic Lachlainn ....(Uig ? Lewis)
Dòmhnall mac Iain mhic Fhearchair mhic Iain Ghlais........(Lewis)
Iain glas mhic Iain mhic Coinnich Oighre (?)
searbhantan Thorcail ....MhicLeòi(Lewis ?)
Uilleam macEachainn Ruaidh ann an Loch Bhraoin ....(Loch Broom)
Alasdair macDhòmhnaill mhic Iain Dhuibh ann an sin........(Loch Broom)
Tormat Coyr[62] (?) mhic Iain mhic Aoidh (?) ann am Pabail
ann an Leòdhas........(Bayble, Lewis)
Gillechallum mac Nèill mhic Fhearchair ann an sin ....(Bayble, Lewis)
Ailean mac Gillechallum mhic Thormoid mhic Iain duibh anns an aon àite
Tormod mhic Iain duibh ann an sin........(Bayble, Lewis)
Iain mac Thormoid mhic Iain duibh anns an aon àite (?)........
Alasdair mhic Dhòmhnaill Gallaich[63] ann an _______ ....(Lewis?)
Aonghas mac Mhurchaidh mhic Dhòmhnaill ann an Leòdhas ....(Lewis)
Coinneach mac Iain mhic Eachainn, fear-frithealaidh Thorcail MhicLeòid[64]

---

61 Denoun a common name in Easter Ross at this time. R.J. Adam, ed., *Calendar of Fearn* (Edinburgh, 1991) 79-82.

62 This 'T' in 'Tormat' could actually represent 'C,' giving an alternative reading of 'Cormac' (Tormod / Norman) However the presence of an 'h' after the first initial letter is problematic. 'Coyr' remains a puzzle.

63 One possibility is that Gallach was a nickname meaning a native of Caithness.

64 Translated here as 'fear-frithealaidh' or attender, however, more likely as bodyguard ? perhaps even foster brother. cf. 'household men' accompanying Torcail dubh Macleod when he raided Easter Ross in 1599. RPCS vi, 84; P. Parkes,'Celtic Fosterage: Adoptive Kinship and Clientage in Northwest Europe.' (359-395) *in Comparative Studies in Society and History*, 48/2 (2006) 377-8, note 37.

Appendix C:
Family tree: Macleod relationships

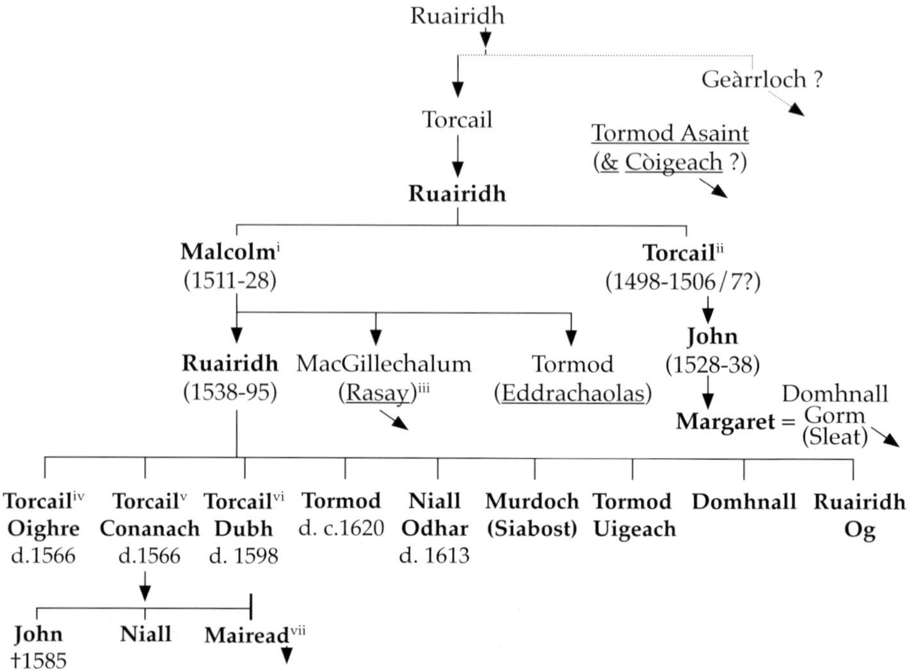

i Malcolm married Christina, daughter of Urquhart of Cromartie

ii Katherine Campbell daughter of Argyll, married Torcail Macleod, c. 1498. Torcail married secondly the widow of Donald of Sleat. This woman was a daughter of John Cathanach of Islay. By his second wife, Torcail had a son who succeeded him. John McTorcail and Domhnall Gruamach of Sleat were thus half brothers through their mother. Domhnall Gruamach's son, Dòmhnall Gorm, married John's daughter, Margaret.

iii MacGillechaluim of Raasay, "Malcolm Macleod's son" (c.1513). W.C. Mackenzie, *History of the Outer Hebrides* (Paisley, 1903) 125; also known as 'Calum Garbh.' A. Nicolson, *History of Skye* (2nd ed., Ard Bhearnasdil, 1995) 291. W. Matheson, 'The Macleods of Lewis,' TGSI 51, 331.

iv Torcail Oighre's mother was Barbara Stewart, sister to Lord Methven (Ruairidh's second - ? – wife)

v Torcail Conanach's mother was the sister of Kenneth Mackenzie of Kintail, Janet – Ruairidh's first wife. Torcail Conanach married Margaret, a daughter of MacDonald of Glengarry.

vi Torcail Dubh (executed 1597/8) and Tormod (died in exile, c. 1620) were from Ruairidh's third wife, in the 1570s. to a daughter of Maclean of Duart.

vii Niall Odhar, Murchadh (Siabost), Tormod Uigeach, Dòmhnall and Ruairidh Òg all illegitimate sons of Ruairidh, the last chief.

viii 'Mairead Ni Leoid' married Ruairidh Mackenzie, tutor of Kintail, who took the title 'of Coigeach' in right of his wife and took possession of Còigeach in right of his own ability (and Mackenzie power) to do so. His descendants were the Mackenzie earls of Cromartie. Mairead's brother Niall died young of a fever, leaving Mairead as sole surviving heir to the Macleod of Lewis inheritance.

For further details on this family see A. Morrison, & D. Mackinnon, The Macleods- The Genealogy of a Clan (Five Parts, Edinburgh, Clan Macleod Societies, 1968-1976).

MÀIRI NIGHEAN ALASDAIR RUAIDH

Anne Frater

Who was Màiri nighean Alasdair Ruaidh? When was she born? Where did she live? When did she die? The answer to all of these questions is the same… it depends on who you ask!

We could even ask the question "*Was* Màiri nighean Alasdair Ruaidh?", as some would have us believe that even the name was not her own.

Her name is recorded in some traditions as Fionnghal, with Màiri being the name of the woman who accompanied her on her travels, putting tunes to, and singing, the songs that Fionnghal composed. However, it is possible that the confusion arises from the patronymic *Nighean Alasdair Ruaidh*, and not from the singing companion, even if she did exist. Fionnghal nighean Alasdair Ruaidh was a poetess from the north of Skye, whereas Màiri nighean Alasdair Ruaidh was from Harris, although she may have spent some of her life at Dunvegan. It is not improbable that there were two red-haired Alasdairs belonging to the Clan MacLeod, living at roughly the same time on different islands, both of whom had daughters who composed songs, and thus the doubt over the name of Màiri nighean Alasdair Ruaidh can be dispelled quite convincingly. James Carmichael Watson tells us that Màiri was reputed to be related to the chief of the clan, and adds:

> "…in Bernera of Harris it is even said that Sir Norman's regard for her was due to his knowing that her blood was not inferior to his own." (Watson:1965, p. xii)

This is corroborated to some degree by Martin Martin, in his notes on Hiort in his Description of the Western Islands of Scotland. Watson tells us that Màiri's brother Neil was MacLeod's factor for St. Kilda (1965, p. xvii), while Martin elaborates:

> "The isle is the Laird of MacLeod's property…he bestows the isle upon a cadet of his name, whose fortune is low, to maintain his family, and he is called steward of it." (Martin:1999, p. 175)

In his *Late Voyage to St. Kilda*, Martin names the steward as Alexander Macleod, who, given the date of Martin's visit in 1697, was possibly a nephew of Màiri's.

Màiri was born in Rodel in the south of Harris. She remembered Sir Ruairidh Mòr Macleod, who died in 1626, and his name frequently crops up in her songs. It appears that she was fostered for a time in Uilinnis in Skye as a young girl, and that one of Ruairidh Mòr's milkmaids was her foster-mother, or muime. If this is true, we could say that she was born around the year 1615. She was still living in 1705, when she composed an elegy for Sir Norman MacLeod of Berneray, who died in that year, so she certainly had a long life. In fact, some traditions state that she died at the age of 105.

The life of Màiri nighean Alasdair Ruaidh, and where she spent most of it, is still a matter of dispute. Harris is generally accepted as her birthplace, and also the place where she is buried, but the island on which she spent her adult years is in doubt. As Alasdair MacNeacail puts it [Gairm: 1953, pp. 55-56.]:

> 'Is aithne do na h-uile gum bheil dà àit ag agairt còrach air dùthchas Màiri Ni'n Alasdair Ruaidh – na Hearadh agus an t-Eilean Sgiathanach… Chan eil eileanaich eile ann as còrdte r' a chèile na na Hearaich agus na Sgiathanaich, agus chan iongnadh sin, agus an dlùth dhàimh a bha eatorra le bhith fad iomadh linn mar luchd-leanmhuinn do 'n cheann-feadhna – Mac Leòid na Hearadh. Is e an t-aon nì a chuireadh eatorra, agartas le taobh seach taobh a thogail air dùthchas Màiri Ni'n Alasdair Ruaidh.
>
> Anns an t-Eilean Sgiathanach, tha i a ghnàth air a sloinneadh air an àit ris an abrar an Draighneach, baile-fearann air taobh siar an eilein. Air fad agus leud na Hearadh theirear leis gach aon gum b' e sin ainm an àit anns an d' rugadh i, ged nach eil àit fo'n ainm sin air àrainn na dùthcha no eadhon an eilean eile air taobh siar na h-Albann.'
>
> *[Everyone knows that two places lay claim to Màiri nighean Alasdair Ruaidh. – Harris and Skye…There are few islanders as cordial towards each other as Harrismen and Skyemen, which is no surprise, given the close links due to being for centuries ruled by the one chieftain – MacLeod of Harris. The one thing that could come between them is where Màiri nighean Alasdair Ruaidh belonged.*
>
> *In Skye, she is always named for the place known as Draighneach, on the west side of the island. Throughout Harris, people say that that is the name of the place where she was born, although there is no place by that name in the area, nor indeed in any other island on the west of Scotland.]*

Watson tells us that Màiri's father was said to be from Drynoch, so the confusion may arise from his birthplace being ascribed to his daughter also.

MacNeacail goes on to put the case for the bardess having been born, and mainly resident, in Skye, using quotations from her songs as evidence. This view is supported by John MacKenzie, in *Sàr Obair nam Bàrd Gaelach,* who assumes that Màiri was a member of the chief's household at Dunvegan. The

Rev. William Matheson (TGSI, vol. XLI, p. 18) also favours Skye as Màiri's residence, placing her under the patronage of Iain Breac at the same time as An Clàrsair Dall, Roderick Morison.

The conclusions drawn by these respected scholars would surely convince us that Màiri nighean Alasdair Ruaidh was resident at Dunvegan for the greater part of her life, were it not for the equally impressive arguments in favour of Harris, particularly the island of Berneray, as not only her childhood home, but also where she spent most of her adult life. John MacInnes notes that "there is a persistent oral tradition that she was a nurse, not in Dunvegan, but in the household of Sir Norman MacLeod of Bernera" (SGS 11: p.6), but he qualifies this by pointing out that Màiri "may, of course, have lived at different times in both houses". However, MacInnes provides linguistic evidence for Màiri having been brought up in Harris rather than Skye:

> 'This occurs in the rime sequence of verse one of *Crònan an Taibh*...where the substitution of *sean*...for...*siud* restores the rime. *(Taibh/ ghean/ sean)*. *Sean* is the modern Harris pronunciation of the demonstrative; this is never used in the Gaelic of Skye, nor judging from what little we know of the history of Gaelic dialects is it likely to have been used in Màiri's time.' (SGS 11: p.6)

Of course, the conclusion that Màiri spoke the Gaelic of Harris rather than that of Skye does not prove that she spent most of her time there, only that, as is generally accepted, she was born and brought up there. A more convincing argument for Màiri having stronger ties with Harris than with Dunvegan is given by Alexander Morrison (CMM: 1954), who casts doubt on the information given by John MacKenzie:

> '[MacKenzie] took no trouble to acquaint himself with the genealogy of the MacLeods of Harris and Dunvegan. In 1790, Douglas of Glenbervie, after much exhaustive research, compiled invaluable works on the genealogies of Highland families. These were available to John MacKenzie, and a perusal of them would have prevented serious shortcomings in his own work. It is also equally certain that they might have led John Mackenzie to make a search in the Island of Berneray, Harris, for any traditions about Sir Norman MacLeod, who was the generous patron of Mary MacLeod as he knew full well. These omissions were responsible for MacKenzie's belief that Sir Norman MacLeod was a chief of the MacLeods of Harris and Dunvegan, and that he therefore resided in the Castle of Dunvegan.' (CMM: 1954, p. 134)

Morrison cites the evidence of Berneray man, Alexander MacLeod, "a man of great intelligence and a veritable mine of information on Harris in general and Berneray in particular", who:

> 'was of the opinion that the great bardess was born on the island of Berneray. He was, however, quite emphatic on the point that she was both the nurse and bardess in Sir Norman's household of Berneray. He could actually point out the site of her house which was in close proximity to Berneray House. It is called *Tobhta nan Craobh* and sometimes *Tobhta Màiri*.' (CMM: 1954, p. 135)

Morrison adds to this with some information about Berneray House, the residence of Sir Norman MacLeod:

> 'About the middle of last century the old historic house was demolished, and only a small building survived, now used as a barn...These historic buildings were all grouped together in the district of the Island, known as Baile – a name still in current use. It occurs in the poetry of Mary MacLeod...and on each occasion the late professor James Carmichael Watson translates it as "homestead", but it clearly means the district where Berneray House was located.' (CMM: 1954, p. 135)

The case is then made for Berneray House, and not Dunvegan Castle, being indicated in Màiri nighean Alasdair Ruaidh's *An talla bu ghnàth le Mac Leòid*, citing evidence from Dr. Norman MacLeod which shows that:

> 'both Sir Norman MacLeod and his brother, Sir Roderick MacLeod of Talisker, were born at Baile in the Island of Berneray. Their father, Sir Roderick Mòr MacLeod, must have had a mansion house on the Island at least in the first decade of the seventeenth century.' (CMM: 1954, p. 136)

Morrison goes still further, using the Dunvegan papers to show that:

> 'the mansion house was occupied on occasions as late as June 1630. In that year a summons of reduction and improbation was served on Iain Mòr MacLeod, son of Sir Roderick Mòr MacLeod. Attached to the summons is a certificate by the messenger stating that the message had been safely delivered at "John McCloyd's mansion house in Berneray..."
>
> 'These facts plainly prove that the mansion house in Baile, later occupied by Sir Norman MacLeod, was occupied by such Chiefs of the Clan MacLeod as Sir Roderick Mòr MacLeod and his son Iain Mòr MacLeod. It could therefore, with propriety, be accurately described as 'An talla bu ghnàth le Mac Leòid'[MacLeod's wonted hall].' (CMM: 1954, p. 136)

The occupation of Berneray House by the chiefs of MacLeod does not prove that Màiri was more attached to the family of Sir Norman of Berneray than that of Dunvegan, but Morrison uses the evidence of her surviving songs to strengthen his case:

> 'Readers of Mary MacLeod's poetry cannot fail to notice that a considerable number of her poems – and that the best – is devoted to Sir Norman MacLeod of Berneray, and his son, John of Contuillich... In striking contrast to this is the paucity of poems on the Chiefs of Dunvegan. There is not one eulogy or lament for such fine and noble chiefs as Iain Mòr and Iain Breac. Indeed there are only two compositions which can be connected with certainty to the Chiefs of Dunvegan. These are *Cumha do Mhac Leòid and An Crònan...'* (CMM: 1954, p. 136)

This argument is made all the more convincing if we compare the works of Màiri nighean Alasdair Ruaidh with those of her contemporary, Roderick Morison, the Blind Harper, whom we know to have been a member of Iain Breac's household at Dunvegan. Morison's songs are full of praise for Iain Breac and, in *Òran do Mhac Leòid Dhùn Bheagain*, full of criticism of his son and successor, Roderick; Màiri's songs either ignore these two chiefs, or just mention them in passing, which would hardly be politic if she was a member of the household of Dunvegan. It does seem strange that the main focus for her attention and praise is Sir Norman of Berneray if we are to believe that her patron and benefactor was actually Iain Breac. Alexander Morrison then gives his interpretation of another of MacKenzie's comments in Sàr Obair:

> 'John Mackenzie stated that he had heard one of Mary's poems in which she stated that she had nursed "five lairds" of MacLeod and "two lairds" of Applecross. Professor Watson attempts to identify these lairds. The five "lairds" of MacLeod, he writes "were, it may be, Roderick the fifteenth chief, who was under eighteen when his father died in 1649; his younger brother Iain Breac; Iain Breac's sons, Roderick and Norman; and Norman's son, Norman. The two "'lairds' of Applecross", he continues, "we must suppose to be Iain Molach, who succeeded his father Roderick in 1646, and his eldest son Alexander". In the absence of the actual words of the poem, we can only regard these statements as pure conjecture. Is there any proof that these "five lairds" were "five chiefs" of the MacLeods? After all, John MacKenzie was mistaken in making Sir Norman MacLeod the Laird and chief of the MacLeods. Might not MacKenzie's "five lairds" be the five sons of Sir Norman MacLeod of Berneray – John of Contuillich, James, Alexander of Unish, Norman and William of Berneray and Luskintyre? As for the "two lairds" of Applecross, might not this be MacKenzie's rendering of "Mac Choinnich"? The Campbells of Harris, the foster brothers of Sir Norman

> MacLeod of Berneray, were styled "Mac Choinnich" in the seventeenth century. Professor Watson ingeniously tries to explain the designation of "Tormod nan trì Tormod" to whom this song is addressed. He says that the three Normans were Norman, the eighteenth chief, Sir Norman of Berneray, and Norman, father of Sir Roderick Mor. Clearly this identification is not convincing. The only sensible explanation of the phrase "Tormod nan trì Tormod" is that it refers to a Norman who was the son of Norman, who was the son of Norman. In the genealogy of the Berneray family, we find a Norman who answers this description, and in no other MacLeod family, thereby proving that this lost poem was composed on that family.' (CMM: 1954, p. 137)

The MacLeod Estate Accounts, for the period during which Màiri was alive, give further support to Morrison's claim that she was a resident of Berneray rather than Dunvegan:

> 'They prove conclusively that the Chief of Dunvegan was no "mean tyrant"…Time and again, the searcher comes across…disbursements and gratuities from the Estate to widows, orphans, and "insolvent" persons…throughout the accounts Mary MacLeod, who was certainly alive and was probably well over eighty years of age at the time, is not once mentioned. Surely if she had been so "closely and honourably associated" with Dunvegan Castle as a "nurse and bardess" during the chiefship of "five lairds", she would not be forgotten by a household at once so compassionate and at the same time so mindful of long and faithful service. The satisfactory conclusion is that she had no connection with Dunvegan, and that, as the nurse and bardess of Sir Norman MacLeod of Berneray, she was already well provided for by her patron.' (CMM: 1954, p. 139)

Another of the widely and vaguely known facts about Màiri's life is that she was banished from MacLeod territory at some point. Although most traditions tell of her banishment, neither the reason for it, nor the location to which she was sent, are known for certain. That Màiri was exiled on the orders of the chief of MacLeod is indicated by the information in *Fuigheall* that the news of her exile being at an end came *O Dhùn Bheagain nan Steud*. However, her return does not seem to have been to Skye:

> '...she mentions that she intends to voyage "westwards", obviously to Harris. There is every reason to believe that *Dùthaich Mhic Leòid* was Harris, for in the earliest charters extant the MacLeods are invariably styled "of Harris".' (CMM: 1954, pp. 138-39)

But this does not automatically point to a recall by Sir Norman, as:

> 'the bardess states that she will see MacLeod, the young Chief of the MacLeods, but does not say where. There is no reason to believe that the Chief was at all times resident in the Castle [of Dunvegan]. He could quite easily have been at the time on a visit to Sir Norman of Berneray.' (CMM: 1954; pp. 138-39)

James Carmichael Watson gives an opposing view of the direction which Màiri's journey took:

> 'The question must arise whether her destination was Dunvegan, the seat of the chief, or Bernera, the residence of Sir Norman. The words [Siùbhlaidh mi an iar] constitute the only tangible evidence for the latter, and we are probably safe in accepting...that her passage was to Skye. Dunvegan would be her natural destination, and especially the abode of the chief is indicated by *dùthaich Mhic Leòid*...for Mary is consistent in applying the proper style MacLeod to the chief alone...' (Watson: 1965, p. 131)

Although Watson argues that "the expression...referring to her passage westward probably does not mean that she was bound for Harris", his explanation is not wholly convincing:

> 'So far as we know, she set out for Dunvegan from either Sgarbaidh or...Mull. If from the former, the expression can be taken literally only if we suppose it to apply to the first part of the voyage to Dunvegan by way of the Sound of Iona. If we are content to concede to her a poetic licence, the phrase is as well used of a voyage from Aros as of one from Sgarbaidh north through the Sound of Mull; in either case it can only loosely describe the first part of the voyage, which is of course on the whole northwards and not westwards.' (Watson: 1965, p. 131)

The drawback to this theory is that Màiri, on the whole, was not given to using poetic licence. Imagery and metaphor are used in her work, but her songs are honest and straightforward. If she sang of going westwards, it was probably because she *was* heading west; and if she was going in that direction, her destination must have been Berneray rather than Skye.

That permission for Màiri to return came from Dunvegan, although it was to Berneray she returned, points to the reason for her exile being that she incurred the displeasure of the chief for some reason. How this happened is not known, although there are several theories. John MacKenzie states:

> 'She gave publicity to one of her songs, which so provoked her patron, M'Leod, that he banished her to the Isle of Mull under the charge of a relative of his own. It was during her exile there that she

composed..."Luinneag Mhic Leòid". On this song coming to M'Leod's ears he sent a boat for her, giving orders to the crew not to take her on board except she should promise to make no more songs on her return to Skye. Mary readily agreed to this condition of release, and returned with the boat to Dunvegan Castle.

Soon after this a son of the Laird's had been ill, and on his recovery Mary composed a song which...drew on her devoted head the displeasure of her chief, who remonstrated with her for again attempting song-making without his permission. Mary's reply was, "It is not a song; it is only a crònan."' (Mackenzie: 1904, p. 24.)

Mackenzie does not tell us how Màiri angered MacLeod in the first instance, but John MacInnes provides several possibilities:

'Modern tradition explains that she was given to composing satirical or even obscene songs...Other explanations are that she aroused MacLeod's jealousy by her songs to Sir Norman of Bernera, or that she over-praised the chief's children – a dangerous practice, liable to bring ill-luck upon them. Watson adopts Mr. Alexander Nicholson's view, "that she was among those dependants who suffered expulsion from Dunvegan under the anglified régime of Roderick, the seventeenth chief, and that she was restored at the accession of his brother Norman...it would place her exile late in life, for Roderick succeeded in 1693 and died in 1699." This is a reasonable assumption. W.J. Watson observed that Màiri's *Luinneag Mhic Leòid*, composed while she was in exile, cannot be earlier than 1675...and it could, of course, be much later.' (SGS 11; pp. 7-8.)

MacInnes then cites Alexander Morrison's theory:

> 'that the motive for banishing the poetess derived from the attitude displayed by the Commonwealth Government towards supporters of the Stuart cause, among whom the MacLeods were prominent. [Morrison] points out that after the chief of the clan capitulated, in 1656, Norman of Bernera had to leave for the continent; it might therefore "have been deemed politic to exile such a stormy petrel as Màiri nighean Alasdair Ruaidh as well", for she was Norman's "most outspoken supporter". We have no evidence as to the length of Màiri's exile; it might conceivably have stretched from 1656 to 1675 or beyond. Yet the tone of *Luinneag Mhic Leòid* is not that of a song composed after long years in exile. Nor...do any of the traditional accounts give the impression that Màiri's exile was so protracted...Mr. Morrison's conjecture regarding the chief's motives for banishing her makes good sense. The theory that this was...a political decision can be applied with equal validity even if we think that the exile is more likely to have fallen in the last decade of the seventeenth century. For it is certainly true that

> the political atmosphere which followed the Revolution Settlement of 1689 was no more favourable to the Gaels than that which prevailed during the time of the Commonwealth.' (SGS 11; pp. 8-9)

Rev. Matheson's theory was that Màiri was exiled for composing the type of songs which were the preserve of male bards, rather than limiting herself to the laments and lullabies which women were permitted to produce, but MacInnes does not wholly agree:

> 'It was not...so much because she was a woman composing the "big songs" that Màiri was banished, as because of the content of these songs. In her panegyric poetry, Màiri nighean Alasdair Ruaidh is quite as strong a propagandist for the Gaelic social order as any *file*; consequently, in the political atmosphere of the time, her activities as a poet could be a source of embarrassment to the chief of the clan. But if she confined herself to songs that did not so explicitly celebrate the traditional virtues to be looked for in the clan leaders – such as songs of normal feminine occupations – then her poetry could be explained away.' (SGS 11, pp. 9-10).

From the evidence, I am inclined to agree that Màiri's exile was politically rather than personally motivated, and that she was exiled from, and returned to, the household of Sir Norman MacLeod of Berneray. Given that her exile was not earlier than 1675, it would seem that the accession of William and Mary, and the troubled period which followed, was the reason for her leaving her home. In the songs composed during her exile, Màiri displays no anger or resentment towards her chief, indicating that she was not in his disfavour. She is not anxious or uneasy at the news of her recall, but joyful at the prospect of returning home, showing that she had nothing to fear from MacLeod.

So, this may have resolved some questions about Màiri's life and location, but there is another tradition surrounding her burial which is out of the ordinary. Both Màiri nighean Alasdair Ruaidh and her fellow poetess Mairearad nighean Lachlainn from Mull are said to be buried in a manner, which, in Norse times, was reserved for those believed to have been witches. Why they should have been treated in this way, when the only traditions that have come down to us about them concern their song-making, is a mystery. Perhaps they were considered to have infringed on the domain of the bards, especially by daring, as women, to compose panegyric verse. The hereditary bards are thought to have been the descendants of the druidic order (Bergin: 1970, p. 9), and certain types of verse were credited with having magical powers; so the idea that these two bardesses had some kind of supernatural influence may have arisen from them composing the same kind of poetry as that produced by the bards. They may have been condemned for having meddled in a type of poetry that was considered to be a male preserve, or there could be another reason, more closely linked with the women themselves, as John MacInnes tells us:

> 'Màiri never married; nor, according to some traditions, did Maighread. This in itself is at least eccentric in that kind of society. Both of them, it is said, went around accompanied by a woman who seems to have acted as an assistant, one of whose functions was to make up choruses of vocables, or to set her mistress' song to a melody. Both women, it is said…were buried face-downwards…
>
> There is…[a] tradition which may have a bearing on the matter. Long ago in the Islands, it is said, if a boat went missing, a wise woman was consulted. She was of mature years, unmarried, strong-minded, and she, too, had an assistant. The woman went to sleep, and while she slept, her spirit went out to search for the missing boat. But, if the wind changed while she was asleep, she lost her reason.
>
> Now this seems to be a fairly straightforward description of a Shamanistic trance and the recovery of hidden knowledge. May it be that some vestige of the poet-seer's practices lingered on in Scotland into the eighteenth century?'
>
> (Nicolaisen: 1968; p. 41).

Màiri nighean Alasdair Ruaidh certainly met the criteria required for a *bean-fiosaich'* as described above. Maybe this respected poetess was given the burial of a witch in order to prevent her spirit from walking after she died. However, if it was due to such a superstition that she was buried face-downwards, it is surprising that this is not related in the oral tradition, especially since she was such a prolific and popular bardess. We can only speculate as to the truth of the tradition regarding the way in which she was buried. Perhaps it was on her own instruction, as one tradition states, "[Gus] beul na brèige a chumail dùinte". (Watson: 1965, p. xix)

Whatever the truth of the matter, it seems that for every theory posited about the life of Màiri nighean Alasdair Ruaidh, from her birthplace, to her home, to the manner of her burial, there is a counter-theory, based on different evidence, and coming to a different conclusion. Maybe one day a piece of evidence will be found to definitively answer all the questions, but until then the debate goes on…

Bibliography:

J C Watson, *The Gaelic Songs of Mary Macleod*, Edinburgh 1965

M Martin, *A Description of the Western Islands of Scotland, Circa 1695*, Edinburgh 1999

M Martin, *A Late Voyage to St. Kilda*, Edinburgh 1999

Gairm Magazine, No. 5, Am Foghar 1953.

John MacKenzie, *Sàr Obair nam Bàrd Gaelach*, Edinburgh 1904

Transactions of the Gaelic Society of Inverness (TGSI), vol. XLI

Scottish Gaelic Studies (SGS), vol. 11

Clan MacLeod Magazine (CMM), 1954

O. Bergin, *Irish Bardic Poetry*, Dublin 1970

W F H Nicolaisen (ed.), *Proceedings of the Third International Congress of Celtic Studies*, Edinburgh 1968

(Cailean Maclean)

View from Elgol in Skye

(John Randall)

View from Trotternish, Skye, looking across the Minch to Lewis and Harris

(John Randall)

Traditional crofting housing in Staffin, Skye

(John Randall)

Lemreway in Lewis, a modern day crofting landscape

(John Randall)

View from South Lochs, Lewis, looking towards Trotternish in Skye beyond the Shiants

(Cailean Maclean)

Sunset over Skye

MIGRATION LINKS BETWEEN SKYE AND THE OUTER HEBRIDES

Bill Lawson

The Problem

I am a great believer in having a factual basis to start from, so I started research for this talk by checking all the entries in the 1851 census for all the Skye Parishes for people born in the Outer Hebrides – and was really surprised by the number I found – in the whole of Skye, other than teachers ministers etc., there were only nineteen households where one or other of the spouses was born in Lewis, Harris, Uist or Barra – and most of these were of Harris descent, living around Dunvegan.

This is strange – with all the historical links between Skye, Harris and the Uists, I would have expected to find much more movement of families between the island areas, but on looking more closely, I think that a pattern does emerge, and it is a pattern determined by the tacksman system, and its collapse.

One of the Hearaich in Skye in 1851 was Alexander Ross of Kensalroag, a son of Donald Ross of Ruisigearraidh in Bearnaraigh. All the Rosses in Harris are descended from a William Ross, who came as maor (assistant factor) in the early 1700s and lived at Roghadal – and he came originally from Skye.

The link, of course, is through the MacLeod chiefs of Harris and Dunvegan. So long as travel was mainly by sea, it was no distance from Dunvegan to Roghadal, and so long as rents were paid mainly in kind, there had to be constant traffic to and fro. A rental of Harris in 1680 shows 22 tenants in Roghadal, in which two names, Angus MacCumra – Montgomery – and John Dingwall, are definitely Skye names, and another, MakCoill Itrawe, has been suggested by Alick Morrison as mac Dhomhnaill an t-Srath – MacDonald from Strath. There are no Montgomeries in Harris since then – though, as I will suggest later, there could well be a Lewis connection – and there are no Dingwalls either, though there is a family in North Uist still, who may be connected.

Tacksmen

So long as the tacksmen – holders of large farms – held their lands on the strength of their relationship to the MacLeods in Dunvegan or the MacDonalds in Sleat, there was far more mobility across the Minch, if only because a lack of suitable marriage partners of the right social class meant that families had to make links further afield from their own area.

When Mary MacLeod, heiress of Dunvegan, married Duncan Campbell of Auchinbreck, it was expected that families of Campbells would come across to Skye and Harris to keep an eye on the rights of her family, and so we have the establishment of the Campbell tacksman families in Srannda and later Scalpaigh. If a tacksman family died out, or fell out of favour, other tacksman would be moved in to take their place, again creating a mobility of families So also the clann Alasdair Ruaidh MacLeods had tacks in Ullinish and in Pabaigh of Harris, before becoming stewards of St Kilda – and hence the argument over where Màiri ni'n Alasdair Ruaidh was born – her family had both tacks at various times.

As tacksmen moved around the relatively small number of valuable tacks, they would take with them their officials – ground officers, grieves, herds etc., and this created a mobility of families. But when the tacksman system collapsed in the eighteenth century, and farms were leased on purely commercial consideration, this movement slowed down, and by the time I had been looking at, in the census of 1851, it had virtually stopped.

We can see this changing pattern when we turn to look at Skye families in the Outer Isles; we can start with some who went there as estate officers. The Shaws in Bearnaraigh, claim to have come to Skye from Rothiemurcus in the time of Ruairidh Mor of Dunvegan, and from there Donald Shaw – Domhnall mac Iomhair – came to Bearnaraigh as maor for Donald MacLeod, the Old Trojan. Several of these Shaws married into the Rosses whom we mentioned already; some moved across to Harris, where the name is still found, but most remained for a time in Bearnaraigh, then emigrated to Cape Breton.

A similar origin is claimed for the MacKinnons in Barra – their ancestor Finlay MacKinnon, born about the 1750s, is said to have come from Elgol in Skye as maor to MacNeil of Barra, and he has a great number of descendants around Tangasdal and the west coast of Barra. Another MacKinnon family, for a time on the island of Theallasaigh, between Barra and Eiriosgaigh, claim that their ancestor, John MacKinnon, of about the same age as Finlay the Maor, was mac Chaluim mhic Mhurchaidh mhic Fhearguis, and that he also came from Elgol to Barra, which could supply a clue to the earlier history of Finlay Maor.

A family who had come to South Uist from Skye at an earlier date were the Martin brothers from Sleat, Dougall and Demric. A move direct from Protestant MacDonald Sleat to Roman Catholic Clanranald is rather strange, so perhaps they were in North Uist for a time, or else Clanranald brought them to South Uist for a particular purpose – tradesmen or the like.

North Uist, belonging to the MacDonalds of Sleat, had of course strong connections with the MacDonald lands in the north of Skye, again mainly through tacksmen and their empl.oyees. One such family, no longer represented in North Uist, were the Lamonts, one of whom had the inn at Trumaisgearraidh.

I remember doing genealogical research for Mary Jane Lamont, the singer from Cape Breton, on her first singing tour in Scotland, and Mary Jane, who had been fed the all too prevalent myth that no-one in the Hebrides ever moved home except as the result of a Clearance, was rather mortified to find that her ancestor had come to Uist as a rent collector for MacDonald of Sleat!

About the same time Malcolm MacAskill came from Rudh' an Dunain to the Isle of Heisgeir, presumably to kill seals, as he is remembered as Calum nan Ron. He later moved to Solas, from where his sons moved to Loch Euphort and then to Australia.

Another early emigrant from Skye to North Uist was Donald Dingwall – Domhnall mac Sheorais – from Dunvegan, though the family presumably did come from Dingwall originally. Donald came to Srom Ban at Loch nam Madadh and there are descendants in that area still – Mrs Rhoda Dingwall is one of the most important people in Loch nam Madadh today – she runs the restaurant in Taigh Cearsabhagh – and runs it excellently!

We have already mentioned the clann Alasdair Ruaidh of Pabaigh and St Kilda. In 1773 Alexander MacLeod of Pabaigh was one of the many tacksmen to emigrate to Carolina, and the tack there was taken over by William MacNeil, son of Roderick MacNeil, merchant in Dunvegan – who was presumably from a Barra family, as there is a complaint to MacLeod from the Church "that MacNeil, his vintner, is a Papist"

The Isle of Bearnaraigh, between Harris and North Uist, always had close links with the MacLeods, especially in the days of Sir Norman MacLeod of Bearnaraigh and the bardess Màiri ni'n Alasdair Ruaidh. One of the groups of MacAskills there claimed descent from the Captain of MacLeod's birlinn and the family of Rudh' an Dunain, but MacAskill was also an old name on the Island of Pabbay and on the whole of the western machair of Harris, from where most of them were cleared to Cape Breton. Another MacAskill family there are descended from Padruig Ruadh Taillear from Glendale.

On mainland Harris, the farm of Srannda was held by the Campbells, who also had farms in Roag area, so it is hardly surprising that there were families of Skye origin in Srannda and the surrounding area – Martins, MacDermids, Gillieses and MacSweens.

In the 1780s, Captain MacLeod of Bearnaraigh, who had recently bought Harris from his Dunvegan cousins, set up a chain of fishing and kelp stations in the Bays of the east coast of Harris, and brought in workers from all over the islands and the north-west of Scotland. The MacSweens came then to Caolas Stocinis, and from there to Scalpaigh and the MacKinnons to Leacli and then Holm at Steornabhagh.

Teachers

Another group, who by the nature of their work, were mobile around the Islands were the school-teachers and missionaries. Andrew Noble, the teacher and hymn-writer, appears in 1851 in Boreraig, though he later went to Milovaig in Glendale, and he also has a Harris connection. His father Thomas Noble was a missionary teacher in the Isle of Pabaigh, and Andrew was born there in 1823. Rev John MacDonald of Ferintosh paid a visit to Pabaigh in 1830, on his way to Hiort, and presented Gaelic New Testaments to Noble's school pupils. In 1846 Pabaigh was cleared of all its people, many of whom went to Cape North in Cape Breton, and when we were there some years ago, we were given a copy of the fly-leaf of a Gaelic testament presented to one of Noble's pupils then.

Moving in the opposite direction was Malcolm Gillies from Kilmuir, who came as a schoolteacher to several posts in the Islands – Geocrab and Leacli in Harris and Cladach a' Bhaile Shear and Malacleit in Uist. He named a son Frederick after Captain Thomas, the marine surveyor – and all the Fredericks in North and South Uist derive their name from him.

The tacksman system was already showing strains before the rebellion of 1745, but the financial problems encountered by most clan estates thereafter led to its complete collapse, and we enter the period of farms, where the farmer held his land solely because of his ability to pay the rent, and not for any family reasons.

Farmers

The best known of the Skye Farmers on North Uist was James Thomas MacDonald of Lyndale in Skye, who took over the farm of Baile Raghaill. Seumas Bhaile Raghaill is probably best known now for the story of the double elopement of his daughter Jessie, first from Baile Raghaill and then from her uncle's house in Roghadal. Jessie was engaged to marry Donald MacDonald of Mogstat in Skye, who was an assistant factor on North Uist. Unfortunately Donald was dismissed, and his job given to Patrick Cooper, an older man from Aberdeen, and Seumas Bhaile Raghnaill expected Jessie to marry him instead! Jessie was having none of that, and she sent word to Donald to come for her, climbed out of the window at Baile Raghaill and ran away with him to Loch na Madadh, where he had a boat, the *Eliza* waiting. They sailed off into a storm, and had come ashore in Harris where Jessie's uncle John MacDonald was factor at Roghadal – am Baillidh Domhnallach. He took Jessie to Roghadal and sent Donald away – to Skye, where he got another boat, the *Eliza Clow*, came to Roghadall, broke into the big house with some Harris friends, and took Jessie away again. This time they were successful, married on the mainland and eventually went off to Australia. The whole episode was the subject of a court case in Loch nam Madadh – and one part of the evidence then given fascinates me. One of the party breaking into Roghadal was reported as having been shouting in a foreign language, and it was explained that he had been for a time in Canada with the Hudson's Bay Company. There is something about the idea of the elopement of a Uist girl and a Skye man from a Harris house being accompanied by shouting – and no doubt swearing – in what was probably the Cree Nation tongue!

But it does also make the point of why there was so little movement from the Outer Isles to Skye in that period – people's attention was drawn in the opposite direction – to Canada. If people were moving in order to better themselves, the prospects across the Atlantic were better than across the Minch – and if they were being forced to leave, Canada was the place of choice of those moving them. At the same time, those who were leaving Skye had come to look more towards the mainland, and from admittedly only a sample from the census of Glasgow in 1851, I get the impression that there was quite a large settlement there from Skye, and virtually none from the Outer Isles.

Another Nicolson family of farmers from Skye is worth mentioning in passing – John Nicolson and then his widow had the farm of Kilbride at South Lochboisdale, before returning to Stein in Skye in the late 1850s. Their daughter Margaret, was married to a Charles Lillia from Finland – which explains why there was a Carl Gregoriev Nicolson Lillia born at Kilbride in 1843!

Norman MacLeod from Kilmuir in Skye, who married Sarah Gillies, daughter of Eoghann Drobhair there, was for a time on the islands of Heisgeir, before becoming the farmer of Griminis in Benbecula, and this makes another point – that the droving of stock through Skye to the mainland fairs facilitated marriage contacts being made along the routes.

With the farmers came their shepherds and farmworkers, and since the introduction of sheep-farming came earlier to Skye than to the Outer Isles, it follows that most of the shepherds coming into Barra, the Uists and Harris came there from, or at least through, Skye.

Barra

As communities were cleared in Barra to make way for sheep farms, we see shepherds being brought in there. Murdo Cameron from Bracadale became shepherd on the Isle of Sanndray, while Robert Grieve from Skye became shepherd on Vatersay. Grieve, of course, is not a Skye name, and when we look at the places of birth of his children, we see that the eldest were born at Strathglass, and others on Raasay. So here we have a fairly common pattern of shepherd families, often originally from the Scottish Borders, moving into the Highlands as the sheep-farms spread there, and following them across to the islands. Robert Grieve's family settled in Barra, but his son David moved to Corodal at the back of the Beinn Mhor in South Uist, and from there to Loch Sgioport.

South Uist

Much the same pattern is repeated in South Uist; as the people were moved out from the east coast, the shepherds moved in, many of them from Skye – John MacAskill from Bracadal at Caolas Staolaidh, David Grieve whom we mentioned already at Corodal, Alasdair Campbell from Duirinish at Uisinis, John Bethune at Teillisdal. The latter is a good example of how names are changed in official records – he appears as Beaton, Bethune and Paton. According to oral tradition, he was Iain mac Fhearchair mhic Iain mhic Dotair Neill, of the Beatons who were for generations physicians to the Lords of the Isles, but all this history was thrown away to make a fake Norman-French ancestry for the family!

Another Skye family in South Uist were the Nicolsons from Stein in Waternish, who came first to Dun Gainmheachadh in Benbecula and then as a grieve at Stadhlaigearraidh. Murdo Nicolson and most of his family settled eventually in Iochdar, but one son, James, became the lock-keeper at the sluices controlling the out- flow from Loch Bi into Loch Sgioport.

In South Uist and Benbecula, there was a double stream of movement, with families from Protestant North Uist taking over many of the best crofts in these originally Roman Catholic islands. Neil MacSween, son of Norman MacSween from Gearry in Waternish, provides an example of the type of movement involved. Up to 1830 he is in Skye, but then he appears working on the farm of Paiblesgearraigh in North Uist in 1832 and 1835, then his next child is born in Hogha Mor in South Uist in 1857. Some of the family remained there, but others moved on to Lionacleit in Benbecula.

There was also a John MacKinnon in Lionacleit and latterly in Torlum who came from Skye – and since his wife was a Jane MacGillivray, they probably were from Strath. According to family tradition John was mac Eachainn mhic Iain mhic Eachainn mhic Iain mhic Ailein mhic Iain mhic Eachainn, which takes us back to the 1500s, if accurate.

The MacFarlanes of Uisgebhagh, on the east coast of Benbecula, were another Skye family from Duirinish. Donald MacFarlane, mac Ruairidh, came first to Baile Raghaill, then went back to Skye, to Snizort, then came back to Bhalaidh in North Uist, then to Aisgernis in South Uist and finally to Uisgebhagh. It is interesting that this same MacFarlane family included a Roman Catholic Priest, the founder of the Free Presbyterian Church, and the wife of a Governor of Barlinnie Prison in Glasgow!

North Uist

Of course MacDonald of Baile Raghaill brought several families in from Skye as shepherds etc. One of these was Angus MacLean from Brunil in Bracadale, a cousin of Professor Magnus MacLean of the *Literature of the Highlanders*. He later moved to the Isle of Griomsaigh, between North Uist and Benbecula. Of his sons, Alexander was the last tacksman of Solas before it was broken into crofts again in 1899, Donald was drowned on the *Penelope* in 1830, and John settled in Nebraska in the USA!

Another family of Skye MacLeans in Griomsaigh had quite a different history – they went to the Isle of Ronaidh when the kelp industry was at its peak, and then to Gearradh Dubh on Griomsaigh and then in 1863 to the Eastern Townships of Quebec, among the small group from Uist who settled among the mainly Lewis settlement there.

Norman Thomson came from Cosleter in Snizort to work on the farm in Griminish, where he had a family of nine daughters. Like the Rosses in Harris, there are many descendants of the Tamsonaich in Uist, but none of the name of Thomson.

A few families moved in the opposite direction, from the Outer Isles to Skye. William MacLeod, shepherd in Uiginish, came originally from Lingreabhagh in Harris, and was married to Rachel MacKenzie from Seilibost, of a family who came to Harris from Shieldaig as road-builders. From Uiginish, they moved to the Isle of Rum, and were shepherds there for many years.

There were others, such an Angus MacLeod – an Ciobaire Hearach in Glendale – and the Stewarts of Easaigh and Pabaigh in Harris will have brought shepherds with them to Flodigarry, but these do seem to have been exceptions, and almost all of the movement was from Skye to the Outer Isles.

Harris

When the North Harris hills were cleared to make a sheep-farm in about 1810, most of the land went to Alexander MacRa from Kintail known here as Fear Huisinis who brought over shepherds from his farms in Kintail and Skye, among them a William MacRae, originally from Kintail, who had been a shepherd in Bracadal. He was married to Jessie Johnston who had been born in Beattock in Dumfries-shire, but, according to oral tradition, her parents had kept a Taigh Seinnse at Ledmore, on the Ullapool – Lairg Road – and an inn with a bad reputation at that! She had a fight with Mac an t-Sronaich the outlaw, but that belongs to another story!

Another shepherd, Donald Urquhart, from Poolewe via Bracadal, was for a time in Scarista, when the machair villages were being cleared, and his daughter Kate Ruadh used to tell how she was given a penny for holding the horse of the captain of the soldiers who were sent to clear the townships of na Buirgh

Tradesmen

Tradesmen were another group to move cross from Skye as the economy of the outer isles began to develop. A James MacPherson came to an Tairbeart from Skye in the 1850s, and opened a shop there, He died quite young, but his widow kept on the shop, and I remember the old people still referring to the shop as Buth Banndrach Sheumais, long after she was gone!

Then there was a Norman MacLeod from Unish who came as a blacksmith to Harris and married in Eileananabuich,. His first children were twins, and I remember trying to find their birth registrations in 1877 for a descendant in New Zealand. We found the marriage, and the births of the rest of the family, and we found the twins in each census return, but nowhere in the birth registers - I reckon that when Norman went to register the twins, he celebrated so much that he forgot to go the registrar – or perhaps the registrar was like the one in Uist who would not register a child until he had drunk its health – which made for an interesting register on a busy day!

At the time of the building of schools following on the Education Act of 1876, three tradesman Morrison brothers came to Harris from Kilmuir at Dunvegan - Murchadh Clachair, Domhnall Clachair and Rob Saor. John Murdo Morrison of the Harris Hotel is a grandson of Murchadh Clachair, but many of Domhnall Clachair's family returned to Skye, to Sateran, in the 1920s.

Lewis

In Lewis, on the other hand, there were virtually no families of Skye origin – indeed in the 1851 census of Steornabhagh, there are more persons born in the West Indies than born in Skye! A few of the MacRae shepherds and sheep farmers in Uig had passed through Skye on their way from Kintail and Lochalsh. There was a James MacAllister, a fishery officer, who had previously been in Dunvegan, and James Nicolson, of the Nicolsons of Scorrybreck at Portree, came to Aignish Farm as a grieve and settled latterly at Braigh na h-Uidhe, but Lewis's links were primarily with Wester Ross and Sutherland, rather than further south.

Engelbert Oehler, a German watchmaker in Steornabhagh, had previously been in Harrapol at Broadford, but the only other Sgitheanach to make an impact on the merchant community in Steornabhagh was Calum Sgiathanach MacLean, who had come from Sleat as a baker, and whose grandchildren still have the Stag Bakery there, and the Land of MacBeth bakery in Forres.

We mentioned earlier Professor Magnus MacLean, and another relative of his – Mor ni' Mhanuis – was married in the far west of Uig to Murchadh na h-Airde Bige – Murdo MacLennan from Scarp in Harris She is famous in the Islands as having been the first person that the outlaw Mac an t-Sronaich tried to kill! Mac an t-Sronaich was the son of the innkeeper at Garve, who in turn was a son of Rev Alexander Stronach of Loch Broom. Mor ni' Mhanuis had, like many Skye girls, being working at the harvest in Lothian, and on her way home, stopped for a night in the Inn at Garbh. As well as her wages, she had brought a necklace of beads – no doubt cheap enough, but they caught the eye of the innkeeper's daughter. At night the two girls slept in the same bed, and mac an t-Sronaich, who had heard his sister admiring the necklace, determined to get it for her, crept into the bedroom, saw the glimmer of the beads in the moonlight round the throat of one of the girls, and throttled her! Only too late did he discover that Mor ni Mhanuis had lent the beads to his sister to wear for the night, and it was his own sister that he had killed! He escaped, and made his way to Lewis, where he had powerful relatives, and hid there among the hills of Uig for several years, and it was at Ceann Reusort there that he attacked the shepherd's house. William MacRae and his sons were out gathering sheep, but Jessie Johnston and her daughter kept him at bay with her gun until the menfolk were alerted and chased him off – so we have the son of the innkeeper at Garve and the daughter of the innkeeper at Ledmore having a fight in the wilds of Uig, Lewis!

But there may have been a much earlier link between Lewis and, not Skye itself, but Raasay. There are a couple of families around Point and North Lochs with very un-Leodhasach names – MacSweens and Montgomeries. There are two main families of MacSweens, descended from John MacSween in Garrabost, born about 1770, and Angus MacSween in Leurbost, probably born in 1760s. For Montgomeries we have three main groups – one in Liurbost, derived from a Domhnall Taillear, born in about 1760, one in Baile Ailein, based on James, John and Malcolm Montgomery, all born in about 1770, and one in Point, based on John, Malcolm and Murdo Montgomeries, all born in about 1760. Of course there may have been other families who left Lewis before records begin there, but the general picture to me is that of groups of families, derived from a range of possibly two groups of MacSweens and three groups of Montgomeries, and none of these appearing to go back much further than a group born in about the 1760s.

So we have two groups of names, neither native to Lewis, arriving there in a generation just prior to 1760. Both names were known in Raasay in earlier records, and Raasay of course had links with Lewis since both belonged to the Sìol Torcall MacLeods. If we look for a reason for people leaving Raasay at about this time, we have the harrying of the island by Government troops in 1746 after the Battle of Culloden.

There is also a family of MacLeods in Point and Tunga known as Muinntir a' Chaiptein – there are various stories about who the Captain was – even that he was the captain of a Swedish ship wrecked in Point, but I remember being told by an old lady in Tunga that her MacLeods were the Glaisich, and had no connection with the other MacLeods in Tunga,, who were originally from Raasay. Could the others have been muinntir a' Chaptein? We know that Captain Malcolm MacLeod of Rigg was out in the '45 with his uncle of Raasay – could muinntir a' Chaiptein in Lewis have been followers of Captain Malcolm of Rigg?

Conclusion

A definite pattern does seem to be emerging. In the eighteenth century, links between the island groups were fairly strong – Lewis with Raasay, Harris with Dunvegan and North Uist with Sleat – and during this period there is fair amount of inter-migration, especially among tacksmen and their employees. Once the day of the tacksman is past, there is far less mobility, and there are far fewer direct links with Skye, these being replaced by mainland families using Skye as a stepping-stone to the Outer Islands. By the nineteenth century, Skye was looking more to the mainland, and the Outer Isles were looking more to Canada.

In the early twentieth century all this changed once more. With better communications between the islands, movement across became much easier, and in the case of Harris and the Uists, the need to move to Portree or to the mainland for secondary education meant many more links being made between the different communities. There were settlements after the First World War of families from Lewis and Harris in Portnalong, Fiscavaig and Struan, and employment in hotels etc. created opportunities for young people to move across and settle, until today there is little restriction on mobility of families across the Minch.

So it does appear that the situation we began with, in the census of 1851, was a relatively short-term aberration, and that mobility across the Minch was much greater in the eighteenth century, in the days of the tacksmen, and since the later nineteenth century, when social and transport links make communication and settlement very much easier.

WHERE DO PEOPLE SPEAK GAELIC? – SKYE AND THE WESTERN ISLES?

Iain Mac an Tàilleir

When the results of the 2001 Census relating to Gaelic language abilities began to appear in 2004, they were initially received with a measure of delight in that over 92,000 people nationally knew Gaelic. It then became apparent that the number of people able to speak Gaelic (as opposed to speak, understand, read and/or write the language) was only over 58,000 and that Gaelic was continuing to decline in its "heartland" areas, including Skye and the Western Isles. Thanks to modern technology and the accessiblity of the Scottish Census Results On-line (SCROL) website (**www.scrol.gov.uk**), it is possible to ascertain the strength of Gaelic at very small-scale local levels and the age, gender and language-skill abilities of the population. In the Republic of Ireland, the five-yearly census asks about frequency of language use, a question which is absent in the Scottish census, meaning that the figures in the following pages show only that certain numbers of people can speak Gaelic, not that they actually do. In addition, the self-reporting nature of the census may lead to unreliability. Can researchers be sure that the figures are neither too low nor too high? One person's criterion of fluency may not match another's. There are indications towards the end of this article that some parents record their children as Gaelic speakers even though they are only learning Gaelic as a school subject and may be far from fluent. This phenomenon was also observed by Professor Kenneth MacKinnon in his study on the numbers of Gaelic speakers in Perthshire in the 1980s.

Because the Census results in the past were most readily available at Civil Parish level, this level of detail is also used here but in Skye and the Western Isles, as well as over the mainland of the Highlands, the parishes tend to be extensive and cover a substantial number of distinct and fairly dissimilar areas. As a result of this, and again because of the user-friendly nature of the SCROL website, it is possible to identify smaller districts within the parishes and use these as the basis of study. A good example of this is the parish of Stornoway which covers not only the town and surroundings but also districts such as Tolsta, Back and Point. SCROL allows the researcher to investigate down to postcode level in some circumstances, thereby illuminating the situation at a very localised level. This article tends to concentrate on these smaller districts as can be seen in the tables below.

In order to put the position of Gaelic today into context, it is worth considering the situation roughly 100 years ago at the census of 1901. At that time, at least 75% of the population of every parish in the Inner and Outer Hebrides (apart from North Mull) could speak Gaelic as well as every mainland parish in an unbroken line from Appin in Argyll, through Ardgour, Morar, Glenelg, Lochalsh, Gairloch, Assynt and Eddrachillis to Farr in Sutherland with outlying parishes such as Glenorchy, Dalavich and Kilchrenan, and Craignish. The majority of the population could speak Gaelic in the parishes of central Argyll, Perthshire, Inverness-shire, Ross-shire and Sutherland and on the edges of the Highlands in places such as the west side of Arran and Reay in Caithness. Parishes now considered traditionally non-Gaelic such as Cromdale in Moray, Latheron in Caithness, the east side of Arran and the west side of Kintyre had Gaelic-speaking populations of between 25% and 49%. Gaelic was spoken by at least 10% of the population of Braemar in Aberdeenshire at this time and spoken by smaller percentages of indigenous people in parishes in Banffshire, Nairnshire, Stirlingshire and Dunbartonshire. Today, there is no parish on the mainland where more than 20% of the population can speak Gaelic and only thirteen parishes contain populations where over 10% can speak the language. The decline over one hundred years is dramatic to say the least.

The figure of 75% is an important one in that it appears to be the minimum density of speakers required to allow the language to be the normal means of communication in the community and ensure inter-generational transmission. Given the changing nature of society, however, and the omnipresence of the majority language in the electronic media, 75% may well be too low a percentage to ensure the survival of an endangered and attenuated minority language. It is relevant to note that after the institution of the Irish Free State, the threshold figure for official Gaeltacht status was 80%, a level now rare anywhere in Scotland.

Before going on to consider the position of Gaelic in Skye and the Western Isles, some general points at a national level may be of interest:

- 93,396 people can speak, understand, read or write Gaelic;
- 58,652 people can speak Gaelic;
- there are three districts in which Gaelic speakers form at least 80% of the population, with 640 Gaelic speakers resident in them (1.1% of the total Gaelic speaking population);
- 3,510 Gaelic speakers live in 13 districts where at least 75% of the population speaks Gaelic;
- 55.5% of the country's Gaelic speakers live in the "traditional" areas and 44.5% outside;
- Gaelic is the language of the majority in Barra, South Uist, Benbecula (excluding Balivanich), North Uist, Harris, Lewis (excluding the Stornoway area and Shulishader) and Kilmuir parish in Skye.

This last point indicates the main difference between Skye and the Western Isles vis-à-vis the position of Gaelic in both areas, namely that Skye is further along the road towards monolingualism in English and possibly more similar to the adjacent mainland and Argyll islands than to the Western Isles. However, trends in Gaelic language abilities show that the diglossic situation current in the Western Isles is leading to the same conclusion as in Skye. The fact that only 640 people (4% of the Western Isles' Gaelic speakers) live in areas where over 80% of the population speak Gaelic suggests that the days when most Gaelic speakers lived in Gaelic-speaking communities are over and that a further attenuation may be expected. The numbers of young children able to speak Gaelic will be considered later.

Still, differences remain between the position of Gaelic in Skye and in the Western Isles:

- 2,918 people (31.1%) of Skye's population can speak Gaelic;
- 15,781 people (59.6%) of the Western Isles' population can speak Gaelic;
- 54.4% of Skye's population have no Gaelic language skills;
- 25.8% of the Western Isles' population have no such skills;
- None of Skye's Gaelic speakers live in districts where at least 75% of the population can speak Gaelic;
- 22% of the Western Isles' Gaelic speakers live in such districts.

The points above show that Skye has a predominantly English speaking population – most people in Skye cannot speak, understand, read or write Gaelic and only three in every ten can speak the language. The reverse is the case in the Western Isles – out of every ten people, six can speak Gaelic whilst less than three have no Gaelic language skills whatever.

The situation within the Western Isles is not uniform, however, as the table below shows.

Table 1: Gaelic speakers as a percentage of the Western Isles' population.

South Uist & Eriskay	71%
Harris & Scalpay	69%
Barra & Vatersay	68%
North Uist, Berneray & Grimsay	67%
Lewis & Bernera	56%
Benbecula	56%

Even within the distinct island groups above, there are wide variations with the highest percentage in Lewis being 79% in the district comprising Linshader, Earshader, Crulivig and Scaliscro and the lowest at 41% in Melbost and Branahuie. In Harris the range is from 84% in Scalpay to 57% in the district from Aline to Ardhasaig including Maaruig. North Uist varies from 84% in the Truimisgarry / Newtonferry district to 51% in Lochmaddy; Benbecula goes from 74% in Liniclete / Torlum to half of that (37%) in Balivanich; while South Uist ranges from 82% in the Middle Quarter to 59% in the Milton / Askernish district. Finally, Barra is slightly more homogenous, going from 76% in Eoligarry / Ardveenish down to 56% in Vatersay.

The variation in Skye is much more dramatic, with Gaelic as a majority spoken language only in the districts of Staffin (61%) and Tarskavaig / Stonefield (54%). Gaelic is weakest in the area from Luib to the outskirts of Broadford (23%), in Kylerhea (19%) and in Glendale between Colbost and Galtrigill (18%). It is interesting that this last figure is the same as the weakest area in Islay and that the position of Gaelic in Skye as a whole is slightly weaker than in Acharacle and south Applecross and considerably weaker than in Tiree.

Although the position of Gaelic in Skye is more precarious than in the Western Isles, there are causes for concern there too. It might be expected that the language would be weaker in and immediately around Stornoway (44%), but Gaelic has also become a minority outwith the town. In Shulishader in Point, only 43% of the population can speak Gaelic; between Garyvard and Sheildinish in South Lochs only half the population can speak the language and the situation is similar in nearby Balallan. Because of the location of military installations in Uist, only 37% of Balivanich's population can speak Gaelic, but no such presence can account for the low figure of 56% in Vatersay. Despite these and other districts highlighting the language's decline, it is worth pointing out that the only districts above 75% Gaelic speaking ability are in the Western Isles, as below.

Table 2: Districts where at least 75% of the population can speak Gaelic

District	Number of Gaelic Speakers	Percentage of Population
Harris: Scalpay	322	84%
North Uist: Truimisgarry – Newtonferry	106	84%
South Uist: Stoneybridge – Kildonan	212	82%
South Uist: Daliburgh – Garryhellie	208	79%
Lewis: Scaliscro – Crulivig – Earshader – Linshader	66	79%

District	Number of Gaelic Speakers	Percentage of Population
South Uist: Eriskay	133	78%
Lewis: Brue	131	78%
South Uist: Boisdale	427	78%
Harris: West Side	142	77%
Barra: Eoligarry – Ardveenish	147	76%
Lewis: Laxay – Soval	136	76%
Lewis: Ness	1179	75%
Lewis: Bragar	301	75%
Total	**3,510**	

If we accept 75% as the necessary minimum percentage to allow a district to be considered a Gaelic-speaking community, then the table above goes some way towards answering the question, "Where do people speak Gaelic?", a question which is quite different from, "Where can people speak Gaelic?". Nevertheless, the figure of 75%, whilst appearing high, is considerably lower than the percentages of over 90% which were standard over most of the Western Isles until fairly recently. Furthermore, the figure of 75% means that in a random group of four local residents, it can reasonably be expected that one can speak no Gaelic whilst all can speak English. The implications for the continuation of Gaelic as a community language in such a situation are clear.

The total figure in the table above of 3,510 Gaelic speakers living in what might be termed Gaelic-speaking districts contrasts with the 20,345 who lived in such districts in 1981, and compounding this dillution of Gaelic-speaking districts is a further indicator of decline, namely the statistics dealing with young children. In a linguistically and culturally stable and confident society with the concommitant props of a relevant education system, one expects that children learn and become fluent in the language of the home and community. The 2001 census shows that, even in the Western Isles, such stability is absent and families and communities lack the confidence to impart the language to their children.

The tables below deal with Gaelic pre-school children, those aged between 0 and 4 years, but because the existence of cròileagain and Gaelic-medium nurseries might skew the figures covering the three and four year olds, the tables have been separated to focus on those aged 0 to 2 and those aged 3 and 4. It should be noted that these table cover the four language skills and not only the ability to speak Gaelic, but given the ages concerned, it is assumed that the children in the tables can speak the language rather than simply understand, read or write it. For comparison, all islands where Gaelic-speaking children live are included, not only the Western Isles and Skye.

Table 3: Gaelic-speaking children in the islands aged from 0 to 4 years

Island	a. All children aged 0-4	b. Gaelic-speaking aged 0-4	b. as % of a.
Barra	49	31	63.3%
Benbecula	84	30	35.7%
Bernera	8	5	62.5%
Berneray	3	1	33.3%
Eigg	9	1	11.1%
Eriskay	5	2	40.0%
Grimsay	7	5	71.4%
Islay	181	5	2.8%
Lewis and Harris	961	303	31.5%
Mull	144	18	12.5%
North Uist	49	23	46.9%
Scalpay	16	7	43.8%
Skye	477	95	19.9%
South Uist	103	53	51.5%
Tiree	26	5	19.2%
Vatersay	9	2	22.2%

It is interesting to note that the percentage of Gaelic-speaking pre-school children in Lewis and Harris (31.5%) is very close to the percentage of Gaelic speakers among the total population of Skye (31.1%), an indication, perhaps, that Lewis and Harris will, by the time of the census after next, be where Skye is today.

Because the figures in Table 3 could be artificially inflated due to children's attendance at cròileagain and Gaelic-medium nursery schools, Table 4 deals with children aged 0 to 2 where a more accurate picture of home language use might be expected.

Table 4: Gaelic-speaking children in the islands aged from 0 to 2 years

Island	a. All children aged 0-2	b. Gaelic-speaking aged 0-2	b. as % of a.
Barra	33	23	**69.7%**
Benbecula	52	16	**30.8%**
Bernera	5	2	**40.0%**
Berneray	1	0	**0%**
Eigg	3	0	**0%**
Eriskay	4	1	**25.0%**
Grimsay	4	2	**50.0%**
Islay	107	3	**2.8%**
Lewis and Harris	560	154	**27.5%**
Mull	79	2	**2.5%**
North Uist	27	11	**40.7%**
Scalpay	11	5	**45.5%**
Skye	267	40	**14.9%**
South Uist	56	25	**44.6%**
Tiree	15	2	**13.3%**
Vatersay	4	0	**0%**

With the exception of Barra, the figures in Table 4 are consistently lower than those in Table 3. The extremely small numbers involved in certain instances, however, indicate that caution must be adopted before drawing too conclusive inferences. Table 2 does point to the fact, nonetheless, that only around a quarter of homes in Lewis and Harris with very young children speak Gaelic at home, and that only in Barra and Grimsay are very young Gaelic-speaking children in the majority in their cohort. The fact that only 25 children are being raised in districts where they are in the linguistic majority may give anguage planners cause for concern. It is relevant now to consider the possible effect that cròileagain and Gaelic-medium nurseries may have on language use among the 3 to 4 year olds as in Table 5 below.

Table 5: Gaelic-speaking children in the islands aged 3 and 4 years

Island	a. All children aged 3-4	b. Gaelic-speaking aged 3-4	b. as % of a.
Barra	16	8	**50.0%**
Benbecula	32	14	**43.8%**
Bernera	3	3	**100.0%**
Berneray	5	2	**40.0%**
Eigg	6	1	**16.7%**
Eriskay	1	1	**100.0%**
Grimsay	3	3	**100.0%**
Islay	74	2	**2.7%**
Lewis and Harris	401	149	**37.2%**
Mull	65	16	**24.6%**
North Uist	22	12	**54.5%**
Scalpay	5	2	**40.0%**
Skye	210	55	**26.2%**
South Uist	47	28	**59.6%**
Tiree	11	3	**27.3%**
Vatersay	5	2	**40.0%**

Excepting Barra and Scalpay, and bearing in mind the caveat about very small numbers, there does seem to be a remarkable increase in the percentages of Gaelic-speaking children in this age group as opposed to the pre-pre-school cohort in Table 4, leading the observer to wonder whether school-transmitted as opposed to inter-generationally transmitted Gaelic is increasingly featuring in the census returns. This point is worth bearing in mind when looking at the percentages of Gaelic-speaking primary school children in the islands. It is noteworthy that in Table 6, a number of islands appear which were absent in Tables 4 and 5.

Table 6: Gaelic-speaking children in the islands of primary school age

Island	a. All primary school children	b. Gaelic-speaking primary children	b. as % of a.
Barra	115	75	**65.2%**
Benbecula	109	63	**57.8%**
Bernera	22	17	**77.3%**
Berneray	11	5	**45.5%**
Bute	627	13	**2.1%**
Easdale	8	2	**25.0%**
Eigg	15	4	**26.7%**
Eriskay	11	10	**90.9%**
Gigha	9	2	**22.2%**
Grimsay	18	11	**61.1%**
Islay	291	54	**18.6%**
Lewis and Harris	1621	854	**52.7%**
Lismore	19	14	**73.7%**
Mull	227	41	**18.1%**
North Uist	132	89	**67.4%**
Raasay	16	1	**6.3%**
Scalpay	29	26	**89.7%**
Seil	45	4	**8.9%**
Skye	810	369	**45.6%**
South Uist	166	136	**81.9%**
Tiree	78	43	**55.1%**
Vatersay	14	8	**57.1%**

Whilst it is heartening to see that 45.6% of Skye's 5 to 11 year olds are apparently Gaelic speakers, it is hard to see how this squares with the fact that only 14.9% of the island's 0 to 2 year olds can speak the language, and one is again led to the conclusion that the census records their school-learned rather than home-learned Gaelic speaking ability, as in the Republic of Ireland.

If the figures and percentages in the tables are accurate, if self-reporting is a reliable means of gaining information and if the small numbers in some areas are to be taken at face value, the future looks as bleak for this country's oldest continuously spoken language and culture. The Western Isles may have a decade in which to turn around the decline in Gaelic, but the figures in the latest tables above suggest that it may be too late and that the Western Isles is following in the tracks of Skye.

It is a pity to think that, when Gaelic ceases to be a widely spoken community language, the Western Isles (like Skye) will cease to be the central focus of and major contributor to a distinct culture and will join the other remote rural areas in becoming peripheral consumers of a culture originating elsewhere to which their sole contribution can be geographical beauty and folksy, slightly ethnic quaintness.

SPORTING LINKS BETWEEN SKYE AND THE OUTER HEBRIDES

Roger Hutchinson

For hundreds of years, specifically since the Middle Ages, the islands on both sides of the Minch in common with the rest of the Gaidhealtachd shared a number of games, many of which have since disappeared.

Those games included cluich an tighe, which was a form of rounders, and a sport called speilean which was closer to baseball than rounders and involved the placing of a ball on a short piece of wood over a hole in the ground - the piece of wood was hit and the ball would spring up into the air and the player would then strike it with a bat. There were also a number of varieties of quoits called propataireachd, there was a form of pitch and toss which was known as spidean, a version of skittles which was called leagail sheaghdair, and a number of other games, most of which as I said have disappeared into history, chiefly in the course of the 20th century.

The one sport which is of course most identified with the Gaidhealtachd and the Hebridean Islands and which has survived triumphantly into the 21st Century is shinty or camanachd - which probably arrived on the west coast of Scotland from Ireland in the 5th, 6th, 7th, and 8th centuries, and then evolved in parallel forms on either side of the North Channel. The Irish game of hurling has grown apart from shinty over the years, while maintaining the same basic rules - it was always in both cultures a team sport where a small ball was hit at at a set of goals with a curved bat. And that was about the limit of the rules until the 1890s.

To begin this story in full we must go to a couple of fairly important years just over a hundred years ago, 1893 and 1894. By the March of 1894 there had developed over the previous decade a number of shinty clubs. Previously this had been a game which had been played traditionally on holidays, most specifically on New Year's Day, with whole communities involved, and by children all year round throughout the islands and across the mainland. The game which is now known as shinty or camanachd differed slightly from district to district. It had been common in Uist, North and South, and all over the islands. James Boswell had encountered it in Coll in 1773, and it was as common a sport as any that you would have found anywhere else in Britain. It preceded the later popular team sports such as soccer which were codified in the south of Britain in the 1850s and 1860s.

A compulsion grew among the Victorian British to codify their sports, to give them rules and to bring them into order, to transform them from crude and unregulated village recreations into properly organised sports. Shinty was not immune to this, and by the 1870s and 1880s shinty clubs were being formed as opposed to village club teams – so people playing shinty in say Sollas on the machair, and Kingussie by the river, or in Skye or wherever, began to establish themselves into properly constituted shinty clubs.

One of these clubs was established in Stornoway and used to play at the town's Battery Park. Stornoway Shinty Club was established in the early 1890s as a formal and properly constituted body, and there was also around about the same time a shinty club established in Portree. It was called the Portree Shinty and Athletic Club - the athletic bit was dropped and it soon became Skye Camanachd, solely devoted to shinty. Various clubs on the mainland like Lochcarron and one or two others on the west coast were also established - there was one established in Ullapool, one in Lochinver, one in Loch Broom. These clubs became a part of the modern-day athletic and sporting landscape that we all now immediately recognise. In the early years of the 19th century such formally established clubs simply had not existed.

Now in March of 1894 one of these mainland clubs - the team from Strathpeffer which later became Caberfeidh - planned an excursion, a tour to Skye and Lewis to play the Portree and Stornoway sides. But within a couple of months they decided to cancel that tour - they would visit neither Portree nor Stornoway. There was a reason for this. The reason was that in 1893 the shinty clubs of the mainland of Scotland had formed themselves into an association, something again with which we are all familiar with today but which then was comparatively new, the Camanachd Association. A year later in 1894 the Camanachd Association instituted its main trophy, the national Camanachd Cup, to be played between every associated shinty club in Scotland. The Strathpeffer team suddenly had more exciting things to do than play friendlies in Lewis.

This indisputably progressive move, the institution of national competition, without which we may not have shinty as a living sport today, had one unintentional but with hindsight predictable effect: it disenfranchised the game of shinty in the Western Isles. Shinty clubs in the Western Isles found it impossible to compete in the organised games prepared by the Camanachd Association. The game had been played all over Uist with a dry seaweed tangle as the caman as there was a shortage of wood, it would have been played in Eigg on the beach with the tide coming in making the pitch two yards wide and it would have been played on every Scottish island. But following the formation of the Camanachd Association, and the pre-eminence of its competitions, and the fact that those competitions were available almost uniquely to mainland clubs for reasons of transport, only two island clubs were left: one was Bute and one was Skye. Even Skye had some difficulty: many mainland teams refused to travel to Skye to take part in competitive games and Skye had to play many of its early matches on neutral mainland grounds. Those circumstances applied all throughout the rest of the Hebrides from Mull down to Arran.

So from this date, from this year of 1894, the islands of the Outer Hebrides were basically left isolated from the mainstream game of camanachd, shinty or iomain. While in the rest of Scotland shinty began to grow as a well-organised and well-refereed codified amateur sport, with initial difficulty in Skye and in Bute, shinty in the Outer Isles was left in limbo.

Let's now look at South Uist in 1893. A couple of years before, a school teacher had arrived in Garrynamonie from Birmingham. His name was Frederick Rae and he left behind what is now a fairly well known book based on his journals of his teaching career in South Uist.

Fredrick Rae's two English brothers, who were soldiers, arrived to visit him in Garrynamonie, and brought with them a football. They decided it would a good idea to blow this ball up and to have some sort of a game on Daliburgh machair. So they did just that. They went out, the three of them, to Daliburgh machair with this ball. What followed may not have been the introduction of the game of football to the Western Isles, but it was certainly one of the first times that football had been played in the Western Isles. And we can be reasonably certain that it was fairly typical of the way that football entered the Western Isles.

The three men, schoolteacher Rae and his two army brothers, booted the ball around on Daliburgh machair for a while, until they were steadily joined by a few local men. Crofters then started appearing over the horizon in great numbers - his description of it makes it sound a bit like the Zulus appearing over the hill at Rourke's Drift - until there was something like 80 or 90 of them briefly playing this game they had not encountered before and had probably only vaguely heard of. They eventually formed into teams with these three English brothers, the basic rules were taught to them, and a full scale match of football got under way. From that year onwards team sport in the Western Isles took a dramatically different direction from team sport in Skye and on the Western mainland. Football became the dominant sport in the islands from Eriskay to Port of Ness.

The development of football, in Lewis in particular, was assisted by the number of men who went to work in Glasgow, and who picked up the new game of association football. They brought back knowledge of its skills and locally organised football then took off - particularly in Lewis where the Stornoway Football Association was one of the earliest football associations to be formed anywhere in the world. It is obviously younger than the Scottish Football Association or the English Football Association, but there was a Stornoway Football Association before there was any such body in most continental European countries. It was formed in the middle of the 1890s and a number of teams took part in its leagues and its cups. They built their own stadiums, being completely self sufficient - the football grounds that we see all over the island of Lewis have a tradition which dates back not to any central Government or local Government assistance, but were largely community instituted and community built.

A vestigial form of shinty was still played in the Outer Isles in the first half of the 20th century, of course. I remember chatting to the late Rev. Allan Macleod, Free Church minister here in Sleat many years ago. He was from the west side of Lewis, and remembered as a boy playing camanachd or iomain there. He described the game to me, how they had basic camans, bent sticks, and a small ball, and they would knock up a makeshift game between themselves as children. I suggested to him that he had been playing shinty: 'No! No! We weren't, we were playing iomain!" But as an organised team game, as a game which attracted support and local identification, football replaced shinty at an alarming pace in the Outer Isles.

Within a couple of decades, effectively by the turn of the 19th century into the 20th century, the Stornoway shinty club had died and there was no adult shinty club whatsoever in the Western Isles. They were springing up all over the place on mainland Scotland, but in the Western Isles they were disappearing. Internal football competitions - leagues and knock-out cups - became the dominant sport in the Outer Isles. They developed tremendous ability at it, not least, I suspect, because there wasn't much else for young men to do in Bayble, Back and Boisdale but become skilled footballers.

In terms of ability, football had been established on a much smaller scale in Skye and on the western mainland, but it remained under the shadow of shinty.

So there was by the middle of the 20th century absolutely no point in a Western Isles team such as those from Stornoway even thinking of playing football against any opposition from Skye or Wester Ross, the gulf in standard was so high. Just as there was no longer any possibility of a shinty club from Skye or Wester Ross bothering to play a shinty match in the Outer Isles - there would have been no serious competition there.

So we had effectively, for probably the first two-thirds of the 20th century two completely separate, divided sporting traditions. One was shinty based, one was football based. The gulf was remarkable.

I have lived now in this area for 30 years. I came to work here in 1977. I have reported on both football and shinty as part of my job as a journalist, and I was also involved in football here in Skye as a player and as a manager. In 1979, the man after whom this lecture theatre has been named, Donnie Campbell or Donnie Crotal as he was known, a man from Breakish who was a sports fanatic and who worked with me in local football clubs, suggested that we take a team to play a football match in Uist, and we did. I think I stopped counting when it was 10-0 to the Uisteach! We felt we had a decent team here in Sleat, and by Skye standards we had, but by Uist standards we were beginners, the boys here just could not start to compete. So, as had been the case for long before then, there was in the late 1970s no point in having an inter-island competition.

A small but I think significant sporting miracle has occurred over the past 20 years. In the early 1990s a man from Ness called Alistair Dunlop came up with the idea of a midsummer tournament to be played in the middle of June between select sides from Wester Ross, from Skye, from the Uists, and from Lewis and Harris - a four-cornered football competition which first began in Ness on a beautiful midsummer day in 1991. By that time football in Skye and in Wester Ross had developed to a point where some sort of competition with the Western Isles was possible. I have to stress that neither Wester Ross nor Skye have to this day yet won that tournament, whereas Lewis and the Uists have won it regularly, but it has been sustained. It was played last summer for instance in Portree and it continues, now in its 17th or 18th year, as a real revived sporting contact between the islands and communities on either side of the Minch.

The second miracle is not quite so minor. It is I think much more intriguing and much more full of hope - because let's face it football is the international game and eventually everyone in the world will be playing or watching football. But shinty is different since it is effectively only played in one country, Scotland. It has cousins in other countries such as Ireland, and it has even more distant cousins in places like Australia. Canada has a version of the same Gaelic game, but shinty itself is effectively unique to Scotland. Through a series of curious trans-Minch connections, chiefly concerning specific individuals, a bridge has been established once again between shinty players across the Minch.

It would have been the case in the 19th century and before that any young man from the Outer Isles moving to work or marry or to live in or just to visit any of the rest of Gaidhealtachd, from Sutherland down to Arran, would have been able to join in a game of shinty and play it. Throughout most of the 20th century that option disappeared from view.

In the 1950s a man from North Uist called Donald Angie Maclean who had attended Portree High School picked up, as many of his generation did, some shinty while at school in Skye and attempted to re-introduce it to Uist when he went back to teach at Paible. It didn't last for very long, but not long after that another chap from North Uist called D. R. Macdonald, who also had attended Portree High School, married into the family of that well known shinty fanatic and rather better known poet Sorley Maclean. D. R., having moved to teach in Skye, found the Skye shinty scene at a low ebb and took it upon himself to revive the game very successfully. Effectively, D. R. Macdonald from North Uist was responsible for the revival of that Skye camanachd club which went on to win the Camanachd Cup in 1990, some 20-25 years after D. R. had helped to constitute and revive Skye shinty. That was the contribution made by men from the Outer Isles specifically to the game of shinty in Skye, and it demonstrated that the connection may have been dormant but was not quite dead.

But something else happened later, in that the reverse began to occur, largely due to a man called Norman (Curly) Macleod from Lochmaddy. He also attended Portree High School and returned home and established an athletic club in North Uist. Children in North Uist began in the 1980s and into the 1990s to be taught to play shinty. Junior shinty was then revived in North Uist and is still played there.

The biggest and most sensational of these revivals, which brings us really full circle from that March day in 1894 when Strathpeffer cancelled its proposed visit to play Stornoway in favour of its newly established competition matches on the mainland, is this. A native of Wester Ross called Boyd Mackenzie who played shinty for Lochcarron went to work in Lewis. Boyd is shinty mad, he couldn't live without the game. This was in the 1990s, and he couldn't find much shinty left in Lewis to satisfy his love of the game, so he started it up, he started up a shinty club with young people, both boys and girls.

By this time the Camanachd Association had taken on a much more evangelical role in developing or reintroducing the game to areas such as Lewis. Such missionary work is never down to one person alone, but it's worth mentioning Boyd because of the trans-Minch connection we are concerned with here today. So dozens of young Leodhasaich began playing shinty in an organised and modern codified game. It was not quite the village iomain that the Rev Allan Macleod learned to play on the west coast of Lewis in the 1930s and 40s. But the organised sport that we know today was established in Stornoway - a shinty club was revived, chiefly due to Boyd Mackenzie from Lochcarron.

Camanachd Leodhais started off by playing a couple of friendly matches. They didn't get great results but they crossed the Minch, they played against Loch Broom and they began to play. Lewis began to play competitive shinty against teams from the rest of Scotland, against the rest of the Scottish Gaidhealtachd, once more.

In fact - as I look at the clock above us - in exactly 55 minutes time something is going to happen that has never happened before in history. At 3.30 this afternoon (Saturday 5th May 2007) at Peterson Park in the Yokerhill Road in Glasgow, a Sutherland Cup match - a game in one of the knockout competitions organised by the Camanachd Association - is due to take place between two sides. One of them is one of the oldest and best established shinty clubs in the whole of Scotland, Glasgow Mid-Argyll. They have a home tie in the first round of the Sutherland cup against Camanachd Leodhais. You won't perhaps find much mention of this in the national press next week, but it is an historic sporting afternoon.

It has taken a long time, 113 years, but finally that particular sporting link between the Western Islands and the rest of Scotland, specifically the Western Islands and their cousins across on this side of the Minch, is being revived and re-established. It's something that 30 years ago would have been almost unthinkable and was only dreamed about, but it has happened.

While Glasgow Mid-Argyll may just win that match against Lewis this afternoon - the bookies are offering very short odds - the ultimate winner I would suggest to you is sporting links across the Minch, and sport throughout the north-west Highlands and Islands.